*FM 7-22.7 (TC 22-6)

Field Manual
Headquarters
No. 7-22.7

Department of the
Army
23 December 2002

The Army Noncommissioned Officer Guide

Contents

	Page
FIGURES	iii
VIGNETTES	iv
PREFACE	v
CHARGE TO THE NONCOMMISSIONED OFFICER	vii
THE NCO VISION	viii
INTRODUCTION	ix
INTRODUCTORY HISTORICAL VIGNETTES	xii
CHAPTER 1 -- HISTORY AND BACKGROUND	1-1
History of the Army Noncommissioned Officer	1-3
Army Values	1-22
NCO Professional Development	1-25
The NCO Transition	1-32
CHAPTER 2 -- DUTIES, RESPONSIBILITIES AND AUTHORITY OF THE NCO	2-1
Assuming a Leadership Position	2-3
Duties, Responsibilities and Authority	2-4
Inspections and Corrections	2-10
Noncommissioned, Commissioned and Warrant Officer Relationships	2-14
The Noncommissioned Officer Support Channel	2-17
NCO Ranks	2-19
CHAPTER 3 -- LEADERSHIP	3-1
Learn	3-3
Be – Know – Do	3-4
Discipline	3-14
Intended and Unintended Consequences	3-16
Putting it Together	3-17

DISTRIBUTION RESTRICTION: Approved for public release; distribution is unlimited.
*This publication supersedes TC 22-6, 23 November 1990.

FM 7-22.7

	Page
CHAPTER 4 -- TRAINING	4-1
NCOs Lay the Foundation in Training	4-3
Leader's Role in Training	4-6
Other Leader Concerns in Training	4-12
Assessment	4-16
CHAPTER 5 -- COUNSELING AND MENTORSHIP	5-1
Leader's Responsibility	5-3
Effective Army Counseling Program	5-5
Types of Developmental Counseling	5-7
The Counseling Session	5-13
Mentorship	5-16
APPENDIX A -- SERGEANT'S TIME TRAINING	A-1
APPENDIX B -- ARMY PROGRAMS	B-1
APPENDIX C -- LEADER BOOK	C-1
APPENDIX D -- INTERNET RESOURCES	D-1
APPENDIX E -- NCO READING LIST	E-1
APPENDIX F -- NCO INDUCTION CEREMONY	F-1
SOURCE NOTES	Source Notes-1
GLOSSARY	Glossary-1
BIBLIOGRAPHY	Bibliography-1
INDEX	Index-1
NOTES	Notes-1

**This publication is available on the
General Dennis J. Reimer Training
And Doctrine Digital Library At
www.adtdl.army.mil**

Figures

	Page
1-1. Army Training and Education Program	1-26
2-1. Task to Assume a Leadership Position	2-3
2-2. Questions When Assuming a Leadership Position	2-3
2-3. On-the-Spot Corrections Guidelines	2-11
2-4. On-the-Spot Correction Steps	2-12
2-5. General Duties of Commissioned Officers	2-14
2-6. General Duties of Warrant Officers	2-15
2-7. General Duties of Noncommissioned Officers	2-15
3-1. The Army Leadership Framework	3-2
3-2. Teambuilding Stages	3-13
4-1. Task Approval Matrix	4-6
5-1. Characteristics of Effective Counseling	5-4
5-2. Major Aspects of Counseling Process	5-6
5-3. Reception and Integration Counseling Points	5-9
5-4. Mentorship Development	5-17
5-5. Mentorship Characteristics	5-18

Vignettes

	Page
Sergeant Patrick Gass and the Lewis and Clark Expedition	xii
Sergeant James Rissler in the Battle of Shahi-Kot	xiii
Sergeant Brown at Redoubt # 10	1-5
Percival Lowe	1-6
Sergeant William McKinley at Antietam	1-7
The 54th Massachusetts Assault on Fort Wagner	1-8
Buffalo Soldiers and Sergeant George Jordan	1-9
Corporal Titus in the Boxer Rebellion	1-9
Sergeant Patrick Walsh in World War I	1-11
Staff Sergeant Kazuo Otani at Pieve Di St. Luce	1-12
Staff Sergeant John Sjogren at San Jose Hacienda	1-13
Sergeant Ola Mize at Outpost Harry	1-14
SFC Eugene Ashley at Lang Vei	1-15
MSG Gordon and SFC Shughart at Mogadishu	1-18
SGT Christien Roberts in Kosovo	1-20
CPL Rodolfo Hernandez on Hill 420	1-25
SGT Park and the On-the-Spot Correction	2-12
C Co. 3-504th PIR at Renacer Prison	3-15
The Deployment	3-16
CPL Sandy Jones in World War I	4-6
The 555th Parachute Infantry (Triple Nickles)	4-10
SSG Michael Duda in Desert Storm	4-15

FM 7-22.7

Preface

This Field Manual is dedicated to the men and women of the US Army Noncommissioned Officer Corps in the Active Component, the Army National Guard and the US Army Reserve – altogether America's finest fighting machine. Your soldiers depend on your guidance, training and leadership to win the Nation's wars. Wear your stripes with pride and honor. You are –
"The Backbone of the Army."

PURPOSE

FM 7-22.7 provides the Army's noncommissioned officers a guide for leading, supervising and caring for soldiers. While not all-inclusive nor intended as a stand-alone document, the guide offers NCOs a ready reference for most situations.

SCOPE

The Army NCO Guide describes NCO duties, responsibilities and authority and how they relate to those of warrant and commissioned officers. It also discusses NCO leadership, counseling and mentorship and the NCO role in training. Of particular use are the additional sources of information and assistance described in the manual.

APPLICABILITY

The Army NCO Guide provides information critical to the success of today's noncommissioned officers. This manual is for all NCOs of the Army, both active and reserve component. While especially important for new NCOs, this book will be useful to junior officers as well. Every NCO will benefit from reading and understanding FM 7-22.7.

ADMINISTRATIVE INFORMATION

The proponent for the publication is Headquarters, US Army Training and Doctrine Command (TRADOC). Send comments and recommendations on DA Form 2028 (Recommended Changes to Publications and Blank Forms) to Commandant, US Army Sergeants Major Academy, ATTN: ATSS-D, Fort Bliss, TX 79918-8002 or through the Sergeants Major Academy website at www.usasma.bliss.army.mil.

Unless stated otherwise, masculine nouns or pronouns do not refer exclusively to men.

This publication contains copyrighted material.

FM 7-22.7

ACKNOWLEDGMENTS

The copyright owners listed here have granted permission to reproduce or paraphrase material from their works.

Depiction of "To Relieve Bastogne," by Don Stivers, © Don Stivers, 1990.

Excerpt from *Men Against Fire: The Problem of Battle Command in Future War,* by S.L.A. Marshall, © Peter Smith, 1978.

The quotation by LTG Thomas J. Jackson in Chapter 1 is from *Dictionary of Military and Naval Quotations,* edited by Robert Debs Heinl, © US Naval Institute Press, 1988.

The quotation by CSM J. F. La Voie in Chapter 2 is from *Guardians of the Republic,* by Ernest F. Fisher, Jr., © Ballantine Books, 1994.

Excerpt from GEN Matthew B. Ridgway, "Leadership," in *Military Leadership: In Pursuit of Excellence*, edited by Robert L. Taylor and William E. Rosenbach, © Westview Press, Inc., 1984.

Excerpt from *The Doughboys: The Story of the AEF* by Laurence Stallings, © Harper & Row, 1963.

Excerpts from *The Triple Nickles*, by Bradley Biggs, © Archon Books, an imprint of The Shoe String Press, Inc., 1986.

Excerpt from *Top Sergeant: The Life and Times of Sergeant Major of the Army William G. Bainbridge,* by William G. Bainbridge, © Ballantine Books, 1995.

Other sources of quotations and material used in examples are listed in the Source Notes.

Special thanks to CSM Gary L. Littrell (US Army, Retired), SGM Michael T. Lamb, SPC Michael J. Stone, SPC Ryan A. Swanson, and Mr. Roger Smith (3rd New Jersey Regiment) whose generous assistance helped make this manual possible.

Charge to the Noncommissioned Officer

I will discharge carefully and diligently the duties of the grade to which I have been promoted and uphold the traditions and standards of the Army.

I understand that soldiers of lesser rank are required to obey my lawful orders. Accordingly, I accept responsibility for their actions. As a noncommissioned officer, I accept the charge to observe and follow the orders and directions given by supervisors acting according to the laws, articles and rules governing the discipline of the Army, I will correct conditions detrimental to the readiness thereof. In so doing, I will fulfill my greatest obligation as a leader and thereby confirm my status as a noncommissioned officer.

COMMAND SERGEANT MAJOR   **NONCOMMISSIONED OFFICER**

The NCO Vision

An NCO Corps, grounded in heritage, values and tradition, that embodies the warrior ethos; values perpetual learning; and is capable of leading, training and motivating soldiers.

We must always be an NCO Corps that
- Leads by Example
- Trains from Experience
- Maintains and Enforces Standards
- Takes care of Soldiers
- Adapts to a Changing World

Effectively Counsels and Mentors Subordinates
Maintains an Outstanding Personal Appearance
Disciplined Leaders Produce Disciplined Soldiers

SMA Jack L. Tilley
12th Sergeant Major of the Army

FM 7-22.7

Introduction

By CSM Gary L. Littrell, US Army (ret.), MOH

I often think back to when I was a young NCO, a young buck sergeant in 1964 at the ripe age of 19 years old. I remember asking myself what would it take for me to be a great NCO? We didn't have NCO Academies. We didn't have noncommissioned officer guides. We had the experience of our senior NCOs and we had the day to day task of asking **ourselves** whether we wanted to be good sergeants and if so what would it take to make us good sergeants. And I thought the number one thing to becoming the best NCO I could be was to be respected. You see, respect is something that has to be earned. Respect is not issued to you with a set of orders and a set of stripes. Respect is something you earn by taking care of the soldiers that you train and supervise and prepare for combat.

One of the first problems that I encountered as a young sergeant — and I know many NCOs today go through the same trials and tribulations I did — is realizing the difference in being respected and being liked. I couldn't define the difference in being respected and being liked. It is human nature to want to be liked, but we can never sacrifice respect for that. The respect you gain through properly training your soldiers to succeed and in ensuring they and their families are taken care of may not always make you popular, but it will earn their respect. It takes a unique leader to be both liked and genuinely respected. Never confuse the two and never sacrifice respect because you want your soldiers to like you. It is far more important to consistently do the right thing.

You will earn your soldiers' respect by ensuring they are trained in all aspects of their job. Individual training is sergeant's business. I have always had a saying that we as NCOs deprive a soldier of his basic right to live if we send that soldier into combat without proper training. Basic soldier skills are important to all, not just to infantrymen or other combat arms soldiers, but also to mechanics, cooks or clerks – they, too, must be proficient in basic soldier skills. If a soldier goes into combat and these skills are weak, you as a sergeant have deprived that soldier of his basic right to live. He was untrained and he died.

We must never forget that the primary duties of a sergeant are to train and take care of that soldier's every need. A good NCO must know his soldiers inside and out. He must know their weaknesses and strengths. He must know the level of training of each individual soldier and if that soldier can work well with others, especially when they are placed in a very stressful situation – like combat.

FM 7-22.7

Soldiers will make mistakes in training but be careful not to criticize them too harshly for those honest mistakes. Mistakes happen in training — they are supposed to. Always compliment your troops in public, but if you have to correct them on a serious mistake do it in private. A mistake made in training can benefit everyone as long as you don't embarrass the soldier. Figure out what happened and why in the AAR – demand complete honesty – but then correct the mistake and train to standard.

A good leader cannot let a soldier do something wrong and not make an on-the-spot correction. If a soldier does something wrong and he knows that you saw him, he thinks it wasn't wrong because you didn't correct him or that you don't really care about him – either way that soldier is less effective and discipline suffers.

As a noncommissioned officer, we must always lead by example. And just as important we must never have double standards. We can't have a set of standards for ourselves and fellow noncommissioned officers and a different set of standards for our soldiers. We have got to lead by example, always up front and we can never ask a soldier to do something that we can't or will not do. Double standards will ruin the morale of your unit very, very rapidly. Have one set of standards for all and everyone maintains that same, strong set of standards.

This FM has a lot of information for NCOs of all ranks. It isn't the only book you will ever need but it can help direct your efforts and probably point you in the right direction in most situations. You'll see many historical references here. History can teach us much. Read about our Army's past and the NCOs who led its soldiers – you will find that their experience has relevance yet today.

Lead your soldiers with pride. Train them well and care for their needs as best you can. Ask senior NCOs for advice if you encounter a problem you don't know how to solve.

You are the defenders of our Nation and the caretakers of its future.

MEDAL OF HONOR CITATION

CSM (then SFC) Gary L. Littrell (US Army, retired):

In April 1970, then SFC Gary L. Littrell, while assigned to US Military Assistance Command, Vietnam, Advisory Team 21, distinguished himself while serving as a Light Weapons Infantry Adviser with the 23rd Battalion, 2nd Ranger Group, Republic Of Vietnam Army, near Dak Seang. After establishing a defensive perimeter on a hill on 4 April the battalion was subjected to an intense enemy mortar attack that killed the Vietnamese commander, one adviser and seriously wounded all the advisers except SFC Littrell. During the ensuing four days, SFC Littrell exhibited near superhuman endurance as he single-handedly bolstered the besieged battalion.

Repeatedly abandoning positions of relative safety, he directed artillery and air support by day and marked the unit's location by night, despite the heavy, concentrated enemy fire. His dauntless will instilled in the men of the 23rd Battalion a deep desire to resist. The battalion repulsed assault after assault as the soldiers responded to the extraordinary leadership and personal example exhibited by SFC Littrell. He continuously moved to those points most seriously threatened by the enemy, redistributed ammunition, strengthened faltering defenses, cared for the wounded and shouted encouragement to the Vietnamese in their own language.

When the beleaguered battalion was finally ordered to withdraw, it encountered numerous ambushes. SFC Littrell repeatedly prevented widespread disorder by directing air strikes to within 50 meters of their position. Through his indomitable courage and complete disregard for his safety, he averted excessive loss of life and injury to the members of the battalion. Over an extended period of time, SFC Littrell sustained extraordinary courage and selflessness at the risk of his life above and beyond the call of duty. His unyielding will, perseverance and courage remain shining examples of the warrior ethos in action.

FM 7-22.7

Introductory Historical Vignettes

SERGEANT PATRICK GASS AND THE LEWIS AND CLARK EXPEDITION

Patrick Gass was born on 12 June 1771 near Falling Springs, Pennsylvania. By the time he reached the age of forty, he had participated in Indian Wars, journeyed to the Pacific and back with Lewis and Clark, fought in the War of 1812 and displayed extreme valor in the battle of Lundy's Lane.

In 1791, Patrick's father was drafted in the militia protecting the Wellsburg, West Virginia area. Patrick volunteered to go in his father's place. This was Patrick's first taste of military life. He saw little action in the following months and soon returned home, but it was the start to a long military career.

For the next seven years, Gass was not in the military. Instead, he worked as a carpenter until his enlistment with the 19th Regiment in May 1799. Gass became a sergeant and served in various locations until the autumn of 1803. Captain Meriwether Lewis was looking for recruits for his expedition into the Northwest. Sergeant Gass quickly volunteered. His commander objected, not wanting to lose both a good soldier and carpenter. However, Sergeant Gass persisted and Captain Lewis accepted his enlistment.

Sergeant Gass, upon leaving his unit, became a private again. He started the journey with Lewis and Clark as one of a number of privates. The three sergeants in the Expedition were John Ordway, Nathaniel Pryor and Charles Floyd.

As the expedition made its way up the Missouri, Sergeant Charles Floyd fell ill with bilious colic. On 20 August 1804, Sergeant Floyd died and was buried along the river's bluff. Six days later, Captain Clark ordered a vote to replace Floyd. The men chose privates Gass, Bratton and Gibson as candidates. In the first US election west of the Mississippi, Gass became a sergeant.

Sergeant Gass helped shepherd his men across the continent and back. Despite difficult conditions, Sergeant Gass led his men to complete the journey with no further loss. On more than one occasion Sergeant Gass' actions allowed the expedition to continue, most notable when he arrived at camp in time to decide the outcome of a battle the main group had become involved in. The Expedition explored the upper Missouri and Northwest, recording the people, animals and plant life of the area. Sergeant Gass was one of those who kept a detailed journal.

Though now a famous explorer, Sergeant Gass remained in the Army serving at Kaskaskia, Illinois. Shortly before the War of 1812, he joined General Andrew Jackson in fighting the Creek Indians. After completing that action, Gass enlisted once again in the regular army. He then served at Fort Massac in 1813 and at Pittsburgh in 1814. He took part in the assault on Fort Erie and served with the 21st Infantry at Lundy's Lane. Ultimately, he received his final discharge at Sackett's Harbor in June 1815.

At the age of forty, Sergeant Gass returned to Wellsburg, West Virginia to spend the rest of his life. He lived for nearly forty more years, becoming the oldest survivor of the Lewis and Clark Expedition. Sergeant Patrick Gass showed the value of a good NCO – to the future of an entire Nation.

SERGEANT JAMES RISSLER IN THE BATTLE OF SHAHI-KOT -- "THE 18-HOUR MIRACLE"

At 0300 hours on 2 March 2002, C Company, 1st Battalion, 87th Infantry walked about a mile and a half to the flight line in full gortex, poly-pro and full field uniform. They sat in chalk order until their loading time of 0500 hours. Their flight to LZ 13A gave them a touch down time of 0600 hours. SGT James Rissler was a Senior Medic of an Advanced Trauma Life Support (ATLS) team attached to the Infantry Company. According to Rissler, they loaded one of the CH-47s with 34 packs and rucks. The flight was to take them from Bagram Airbase at 4,200 feet to LZ 13A in Shahi-Kot valley to just outside the city of Marzak at 10,500 feet in just an hour's time. Their mission set up blocking positions outside the city of Marzak while Zia forces pushed the Taliban and Al-Qaeda forces in their direction.

The flight left at 0500 hours as planned and touched down at LZ 13A at 0600 hours. When the chopper touched down, the unit hastily split and went off to the left and right sides of the aircraft and soldiers assumed prone positions. Once the aircraft had taken off, the unit immediately started receiving small arms fire. The problem was that no one could locate the direction of fire, so they dropped their rucks and ran up the side of a small ridge. Soon realizing that the direction of fire was coming from the same side they were on, they ran to the top of the ridge to the other side to take cover. Once Sergeant Rissler reached the top of the ridge, an RPG round exploded about 10 feet from him and a piece of shrapnel hit him in the knee.

Once they all got to the other side, the unit consolidated and started constructing fighting positions. Soldiers were placed on a small observation post to the right of the unit, but were quickly targeted by Mortar fire also. The Mortars adjusted fire and the unit took 13 casualties by the time the second round hit. The unit then realized that the enemy forces were running out of the city of Marzak to surround them, which meant that they would now be taking fire from three sides, being targeted by Mortar fire. Sergeant Rissler set up a Command and Control Post at the bottom of the ridge and it was quickly targeted. As the enemy continued to adjust fire on them, Sergeant Rissler and other soldiers would drag as many casualties up and down the ridge as possible, covering their bodies with theirs to protect them as the rounds detonated.

While moving the soldiers up and down the hill, Sergeant Rissler was wounded a second time, taking fragments in the hand. Both times he was wounded he treated himself. Moving the injured soldiers up and down the ridge was only aggravating the injuries; consequently, each time a soldier was moved, controlling of bleeding and treatment of wound started all over again. The Mortar fire would slow down when fire missions were called in from the F-16s and AC 130s, allowing Sergeant Rissler and other soldiers to dig pits in the center of the valley to put the patients in and using dirt or whatever materials found to cover the wounded. All patients were stabilized and the unit lay in their positions returning fire until nightfall.

As night started to set in, Sergeant Rissler knew that it would be getting very cold soon. With the amount of blood lost through the day and the rapid decrease in temperature the patients would probably go into shock. So Sergeant Rissler used tape to repair the wounded soldiers' clothing and covered the soldiers with whatever he had to prevent shock. Then he and other soldiers lay on the wounded patients to maintain their body temperature. Finally, when night fell MEDEVAC could get to the site. The first helicopter received two Mortar rounds and heavy small arms fire. Another AC-130 was called in to cover the evacuation. In all, 25 wounded were evacuated with no fatalities. Around 0200 hours the next morning, Sergeant Rissler and the rest of the unit were extracted.

Chapter 1
History and Background

Since 14 June 1775, soldiers have defended freedom and are fighting on behalf of the American people for various missions. All of our forces – heavy and light, Active, Guard and Reserve – share the heritage of the Continental Army.

The Army's Birthday celebrates this great institution and upon reflection a simple truth arises: there is no greater profession than the Profession of Arms and no greater job than ours – serving on point for our Nation. Thanks to American Soldiers, freedom's light shines as a beacon throughout the world.

Your unit, organization and or installation may celebrate the Army's Birthday and Flag Day together. For example, some have the youngest and oldest soldier attend the ceremony to cut the cake and be a part of the retreat ceremony as the guest speaker explains this traditional event.

The Army has courageously fought our country's wars and served honorably in peace for over two centuries. We can all be justifiably proud of the Army's achievements – a distinguished history of service to the Nation. Ever since the American Revolution, through the trial of the Civil War; from the trenches of World War I to the beaches of Normandy and the island battles in the Pacific of World War II; from the frozen mountains of Korea to the sweltering paddies of Vietnam; from Grenada and Panama to the sands of Kuwait and Iraq and on the plains and mountains of Afghanistan: Soldiers have upheld democracy and liberty and justice for all.

Throughout that history of service, the key to the Army's success is our flexibility and willingness to change, to meet the world as it is – without altering the core competencies that make the Army the best fighting force in the world. You are the best Army in the world. You represent what is most noble about our Nation: liberty, freedom and unity. As a symbol of our transformed Army, you are and will continue to be, respected by your allies, feared by your opponents and esteemed by the American people. Your courage, dedication to duty and selfless service to the Nation will remain the hallmark you, the Soldiers of the United States Army, carry into the 21st Century.

FM 7-22.7

As a leader, as a trainer and as a teacher, the NCO embodies the Army's past, present and future

	Page
History of the Army Noncommissioned Officer	1-3
The Revolution to the Civil War	1-3
The Civil War to World War 1	1-7
The World Wars and Containment	1-11
Post-Vietnam and the Volunteer Army	1-16
Contemporary Operational Environment	1-20
Army Transformation	1-21
Army Values	1-22
Loyalty	1-22
Duty	1-23
Respect	1-23
Selfless Service	1-24
Honor	1-24
Integrity	1-24
Personal Courage	1-25
NCO Professional Development	1-26
The NCO Education System	1-26
Operational Assignments	1-28
NCODP	1-29
Self-development	1-29
The NCO Transition	1-32

For more information on the history of the US Army Noncommissioned Officer, see Appendix C, The NCO Professional Reading List.

For more information on Army Values, see FM 6-22 (22-100) *Army Leadership*, Chapter 2.

For more information on US Army NCO professional development, see DA PAM 600-25, "The US Army NCO Professional Development Guide."

History and Background

HISTORY OF THE ARMY NONCOMMISSIONED OFFICER

1-1. You are a leader in the same Army that persevered at Valley Forge, held its ground at the Little Round Top, turned the tide of a war at St. Mihiel and began the liberation of a continent at Omaha Beach. You lead soldiers from the same Army that burst out of the Pusan Perimeter, won against enormous odds at the Ia Drang Valley, fought with determination at Mogadishu and relieved terrible misery in Rwanda. Leaders like you and soldiers like yours conducted intense combat operations in Afghanistan while only a short distance away others supported that nation's rebuilding and still others fought fires in the northwestern US. Throughout the history of the Army the NCO has been there, leading soldiers in battle and training them in peacetime, leading by example and always, always – out front.

THE REVOLUTION TO THE CIVIL WAR

1-2. The history of the United States Army and of the noncommissioned officer began in 1775 with the birth of the Continental Army. The American noncommissioned officer did not copy the British. He, like the American Army itself, blended traditions of the French, British and Prussian armies into a uniquely American institution. As the years progressed, the American political system, with its disdain for the aristocracy, social attitudes and the vast westward expanses, further removed the US Army noncommissioned officer from his European counterparts and created a truly American noncommissioned officer.

> *"Understanding the history of our profession and our corps is at the heart of being a soldier. Every soldier needs to learn about our heritage and traditions, it is the essence of who we are."*
>
> CSM Cynthia Pritchett

The Revolution

1-3. In the early days of the American Revolution, little standardization of NCO duties or responsibilities existed. In 1778, during the long hard winter at Valley Forge, Inspector General Friedrich von Steuben standardized NCO duties and responsibilities in his *Regulations for the Order and Discipline of the Troops of the United States* (printed in 1779). His work, commonly called the Blue Book, set down the duties and responsibilities for corporals, sergeants, first sergeants, quartermaster sergeants and sergeants major, which were the NCO ranks of the period. The Blue Book also emphasized the importance of selecting quality soldiers for NCO positions and served a whole generation of soldiers as the primary regulation for the Army for 30 years. In fact, part of Von Steuben's Blue Book is still with us in FM 22-5, *Drill and Ceremonies* and other publications.

1-4. Von Steuben specified duties of the noncommissioned officer. The Sergeant Major served as the assistant to the regimental adjutant, keeping rosters, forming details and handling matters concerning the "interior management and discipline of the regiment." The Sergeant Major also served "at the head of the noncommissioned officers." The Quartermaster Sergeant assisted the regimental quartermaster, assuming his duties in the quartermaster's absence and supervising the proper loading and transport of the regiment's baggage when on march. The First Sergeant enforced discipline and encouraged duty among troops, maintaining the duty roster, making morning report to the company commander and keeping the company descriptive book. This document listed the name, age, height, place of birth and prior occupation of every enlisted man in the unit.

1-5. The day-to-day business of sergeants and corporals included many roles. Sergeants and Corporals instructed recruits in all matters of military training, including the order of their behavior in regard to neatness and sanitation. They quelled disturbances and punished perpetrators. They forwarded sick lists to the First Sergeant. In battle, NCOs closed the gaps occasioned by casualties, encouraged men to stand their ground and to fire rapidly and accurately. The development of a strong NCO Corps helped sustain the Continental Army

History and Background

through severe hardships to final victory. Von Steuben's regulations established the foundation for NCO duties and responsibilities from 1778 to the present.

1-6. During the early stages of the American Revolution the typical Continental Army NCO wore an epaulet to signify his rank. Corporals wore green and sergeants wore red epaulets. After 1779, sergeants wore two epaulets, while corporals retained a single epaulet. From the American Revolution to World War II the noncommissioned officer received his promotion from the regimental commander. Entire careers were often spent within one regiment. If a man transferred from one regiment to the next, he did not take his rank with him. No noncommissioned officer could transfer in grade from one regiment to another without the permission of the General in Chief of the Army; this was rarely done. Without permanent promotions of individuals, stripes stayed with the regiment.

> **Sergeant Brown at Redoubt Number 10**
>
> On the 14th of October, 1781, Sergeant William Brown, during the all-important siege of Yorktown, led the advance party, known in those days as a 'forlorn hope,' against Redoubt Number 10 in the British defenses. Sergeant Brown declined to wait for sappers to clear the abatis that ringed the objective or to breach the picket-like fraise that blocked the way up the slope to the British position. Instead, he led his soldiers over and through these obstructions to enter the redoubt in a surprise assault. Using only their bayonets, the Americans captured the position within ten minutes. Sergeant Brown was among the casualties, with a bayonet wound in the hand.

The Purple Heart

1-7. Three NCOs received special recognition for acts of heroism during the American Revolution. These men, Sergeant Elijah Churchill, Sergeant William Brown and Sergeant Daniel Bissell, received the Badge of Military Merit, a purple heart with a floral border and the word "merit" inscribed across the center. In practice this award was the precursor to the Medal of Honor introduced during the Civil War. After a long period of disuse, Badge of Military Merit was reinstituted in 1932 as the Purple Heart and is a decoration for members of the armed forces wounded or killed in action or as a result of a terrorist attack.

Rank Insignia

1-8. In 1821 the War Department made the first reference to noncommissioned officer chevrons. A General Order directed that sergeants major and quartermaster sergeants wear a worsted chevron on each arm above the elbow; sergeants and senior musicians, one on each arm below the elbow; and corporals, one on the right arm above the elbow. This practice ended in 1829

FM 7-22.7

but returned periodically and became a permanent part of the NCO's uniform before the Civil War.

1-9. In 1825 the Army established a systematic method for selecting noncommissioned officers. The appointment of regimental and company noncommissioned officers remained the prerogative of the regimental commander. Usually regimental commanders would accept the company commander's recommendations for company NCOs unless there were overriding considerations. *The Abstract of Infantry Tactics*, published in 1829, provided instructions for training noncommissioned officers. The purpose of this instruction was to ensure that all NCOs possessed "an accurate knowledge of the exercise and use of their firelocks, of the manual exercise of the soldier and of the firings and marchings."

Percival Lowe

In October 1849, a young Massachusetts farm boy named Percival Lowe joined the US Army's Dragoons. Having read Fremont's Narrative of 1843-1844 and other Army adventures, he felt that five years of life in the west would round out his education. Lowe was intelligent, well educated and strong, which made him an ideal soldier for the years ahead.

During the next few months Lowe proved himself as a soldier. He learned quickly how to keep his horse in sound condition while campaigning. He also learned the ways of the Plains and the various Indian tribes that lived upon it. More than anything, however, he learned about the individual soldiers in his unit and how to lead them. He was promoted to corporal, then sergeant and in June of 1851, a little over two years after he had enlisted, Lowe became first sergeant of his company. Two years after he made first sergeant in 1853, Lowe viewed whiskey as the major source of discipline problems for enlisted men. He talked with other noncommissioned officers about this and cautioned each to give personal attention to his men to ensure they were not drinking to excess.

Sometimes Lowe would lock drunken soldiers in a storeroom until they sobered up. Offenders received extra duty as punishment. Lowe and the noncommissioned officers of the company established the "company court-martial" (not recognized by Army regulations). This allowed the noncommissioned officers to enforce discipline, for the breaking of minor regulations, without lengthy proceedings. In the days before the summary court martial, it proved effective to discipline a man by the company court-martial and avoided ruining his career by bringing him before three officers of the regiment.

1-10. Field officers and the adjutant frequently assembled noncommissioned officers for both practical and theoretical instruction. Furthermore, field officers ensured that company officers provided proper instruction to their noncommissioned officers. The sergeant major assisted in instructing

History and Background

sergeants and corporals of the regiment. Newly promoted corporals and sergeants of the company received instruction from the First Sergeant. The first sergeant of that time, like today, was a key person in the maintenance of military discipline.

THE CIVIL WAR TO WORLD WAR 1

The Civil War

1-11. During the 1850's major changes occurred in US Army weaponry. Inventors developed and refined the percussion cap and rifled weapons. Weapons like the Sharps carbine added greatly to fire power and accuracy. The increased lethality of weapons did not immediately result in different tactics. The huge numbers of casualties in the American Civil War proved that technological advances must result in changes to battlefield tactics. Operationally, the Civil War marked a distinct change in warfare. No longer was it sufficient to defeat an enemy's army in the field. It was necessary to destroy the enemy's will and capacity to resist through military, economic and political means. This became the concept of total war. The war required a large number of draftees and unprecedented quantities of supplies.

Sergeant William McKinley at Antietam

William McKinley enlisted in Colonel (later President) Rutherford B. Hayes' 23rd Ohio Infantry Regiment in June, 1861. During the battle of Antietam on 17 September 1862 Commissary Sergeant McKinley was in the rear in charge of his unit's supplies. The men had eaten only a scanty breakfast and McKinley knew as the day wore on that the Buckeye soldiers were growing weaker.

Gathering some stragglers, Sergeant McKinley led two mule teams with wagons of rations and hot coffee into the thick of battle. Working his way over rough ground under fire, McKinley ignored repeated warnings to retreat. He lost one team of mules to enemy fire but did not return to the rear of the brigade until his fellow soldiers had been properly fed under adverse combat conditions. McKinley later was a congressman, governor and was elected the 25th President of the United States in 1896.

1-12. During the Civil War, noncommissioned officers led the lines of skirmishers that preceded and followed each major unit. NCOs also carried the flags and regimental colors of their units. This deadly task was crucial to maintain regimental alignment and for commanders to observe their units on the field. As the war progressed, organizational and tactical changes led the Army to employ more open battle formations. These changes further enhanced the combat leadership role of the noncommissioned officer. New technology shaped the Army during the Civil War: railroads, telegraph communications, steamships, balloons and other innovations. These innovations would later impact the noncommissioned officer rank structure and pay.

1-13. Since its founding on 14 June 1775, the Army normally expanded in wartime with volunteers, with the professional soldiers forming the basis for expansion. The Civil War in particular brought a huge increase in the number of volunteer soldiers. This policy endured to some extent until world commitments and the stationing of troops overseas in the 20th century required the Nation to maintain a strong professional force.

> **The 54th Massachusetts Assault on Fort Wagner**
>
> The 54th Massachusetts Regiment was selected to lead the attack against Fort Wagner, one of the fortifications protecting Charleston Harbor from seaborne assault. Although the battle of Fort Wagner was minor compared to the Civil War's major battles, it clearly demonstrated to the Nation that valor and commitment was present throughout its entire Army.
>
> At twilight on 18 July 1863 the 54th led two Union brigades through the Carolina low country and across a sandy beach toward the fort... As they approached, the Confederates let loose volley after volley of musket-fire into the soldiers. Although men fell left and right, the bulk of the 54th managed to charge onto the parapets of the fort, climbing down into it to fight hand to hand. The 54th was able to hold its ground for an hour before finally being pushed back. But even in the tumult, the 54th's gallantry showed. Sergeant William H. Carney, severely wounded, still managed to save the 54th's battle flag and kneel with it on the crest of the fort as the battle raged around him. When the attack ended, Carney carried the flag to safety. For this action, Sergeant Carney became the first African-American to receive the Medal of Honor.
>
> Frederick Douglass' son Lewis wrote to his sweetheart shortly after the battle, "This regiment has established itself as a fighting regiment... not a man flinched, though it was a trying time... Remember if I die, I die in a good cause."
>
> Although the 54th lost over 50 percent of its men, including Col. Shaw, the glory of the regiment and this battle was honored by the Nation both during the Civil War and in the 130 years since.

1-14. In the post-Civil War era the Artillery School at Fort Monroe reopened to train both officers and noncommissioned officers. In 1870 the Signal Corps established a school for training officers and noncommissioned officers. Because both the Artillery and the Signal Corps required soldiers to have advanced technical knowledge to operate complex equipment and instruments, these were the first schools established. Efforts to provide advanced education for noncommissioned officers in other less technical fields, however, failed to attract supporters. Army leaders thought experience and not the classroom made a good NCO.

_____ **History and Background**

Military Life on the Frontier

1-15. During the Indian Wars period, enlisted men lived in spartan barracks with corporals and privates in one large room. Sergeants lived separately from their men in small cubicles of their own adjacent to the men's sleeping quarters. This gave enlisted men a sense of comradeship, but allowed little privacy.

> **Buffalo Soldiers and Sergeant George Jordan**
>
> African-American soldiers of this period were often referred to as Buffalo Soldiers. The units they served in were the 9th and 10th Cavalry and the 24th and 25th Infantry. These troops provided 20 years of continuous frontier service. They campaigned in the southern plains, in west Texas, in the Apache lands and against the Sioux. Sergeant George Jordan, a Buffalo Soldier, won the Medal of Honor for actions during the campaign against the Apache leader Victorio. Sergeant Jordan led a 25-man unit to Tularosa, New Mexico, to stave off a coming attack. Standing firm against 200-300 Apaches, Sergeant Jordan and his men prevented the town's destruction.

1-16. During the 1870s the Army discouraged enlisted men from marrying. Regulations limited the number of married enlisted men in the Army and required special permission to marry. Those men who did marry without permission could be charged with insubordination. They could not live in post housing or receive other entitlements. Still, nature proved stronger than Army desires or regulations. Marriages occurred and posts became communities.

1-17. Barracks life in the 1890s was simple, with card games, dime novels and other amusements filling idle time. Footlockers contained personal possessions, along with military clothing and equipment. Soldiers during this period maintained handbooks that contained a variety of information, including sections entitled, "Extracts from Army Regulations of 1895," "Examination of Enlisted Men for Promotion," "Take Care of Your Health," "Extracts from Articles of War," and others. In the back there were three sections for the soldier to fill in: "Clothing Account," "Military Service," and "Last Will and Testament." Soldiers carried these handbooks for a number of years and provided an accurate record of the important events in his Army life.

> **Corporal Titus in the Boxer Rebellion**
>
> In the summer of 1900 American troops joined soldiers from seven other nations to rescue citizens besieged in their embassies in the walled city of Peking during an outbreak of violence directed at foreigners in China. On 14 August, when his commander asked for a volunteer to scale the east wall of the city without the aid of ropes or ladders, Musician Corporal Calvin P. Titus said, "I'll try, sir." Under enemy fire Corporal Titus successfully climbed the wall by way of jagged holes in its surface. His company followed his lead up the wall and into the city. Titus received the Medal of Honor.

1-18. The increase of technology which accompanied modernization greatly affected the NCO Corps during the last half of the 19th Century. The number of NCO ranks grew rapidly; each new advent of technology created another pay grade. The Army was forced to compete with industry for technical workers. In 1908 Congress approved a pay bill which rewarded those in technical fields in order to retain their services. Combat soldiers were not so fortunate. A Master Electrician in the Coast Artillery made $75-84 per month, while an Infantry Battalion Sergeant Major lived on $25-34 per month. Compare that with a Sergeant of the Signal Corps ($34 - $43 per month).

Enlisted Retirement

1-19. In 1885 Congress authorized voluntary retirement for enlisted soldiers. The system allowed a soldier to retire after 30 years of service with three-quarters of his active duty pay and allowances. This remained relatively unchanged until 1945 when enlisted personnel could retire after 20 years of service with half pay. In 1948 Congress authorized retirement for career members of the Reserve and National Guard. Military retirement pay is not a pension, but rather is delayed compensation for completing 20 or more years of active military service. It not only provides an incentive for soldiers to complete 20 years of service, but also creates a backup pool of experienced personnel in the event of a national emergency.

NCO Guide

1-20. The Army began to explicitly define NCO duties during the late 19th and early 20th centuries. The five or six pages of instructions provided by von Steuben's *Regulations for the Order and Discipline of the Troops of the United States* in 1778 grew to 417 pages in the 1909 *Noncommissioned Officers Manual*. While an unofficial publication, it was widely used and the chapters describing the duties of the First Sergeant and Sergeant Major included common forms, a description of duties, what should and should not be done and customs of the service. The *Noncommissioned Officers Manual* included a chapter on discipline that stressed the role of punishment in achieving discipline. The manual stated that the purpose of punishment was to prevent the commission of offenses and to reform the offender. However, this section repeatedly stressed that treatment of subordinates should be uniform, just and in no way humiliating.

The Modern Rank Insignia

1-21. In 1902 the NCO symbol of rank, the chevron, rotated to what we would today call point up and became smaller in size. Though many stories exist as to why the chevron's direction changed, the most probable reason was simply that it looked better. Clothing had become more form fitting, creating narrower sleeves; in fact, the 10-inch chevron of the 1880s would have wrapped completely around the sleeve of a 1902 uniform.

History and Background

THE WORLD WARS AND CONTAINMENT

World War 1

1-22. World War I required the training of four million men, one million of which would go overseas. Corporals were the primary trainers during this period, teaching lessons that emphasized weapons and daytime maneuvers. Training included twelve hours devoted to the proper use of the gas mask and a trip to the gas chamber. After viewing the differences in American and foreign NCO prestige, American Commanding General John J. Pershing suggested the establishment of special schools for sergeants and separate NCO messes. The performance of noncommissioned officers in the American Expeditionary Force seemed to validate these changes.

> **Sergeant Patrick Walsh in World War I**
>
> When the United States entered World War I in 1917, Sergeant Patrick Walsh already had thirty-one years of service and was eligible to retire. Instead, he chose to remain with his unit when it left for France. On 1 March 1918, near Seicheprey, Sergeant Walsh followed his company commander through a severe barrage to the first line of trenches to attack. When the company commander was killed, Sergeant Walsh assumed command and initiated an assault that resulted in heavy enemy losses. He received the Distinguished Service Cross for his demonstration of leadership.

1-23. In 1922 the Army scheduled 1,600 noncommissioned officers for grade reductions. Although this was necessary to reduce the total force and save money, it caused severe hardships for many noncommissioned officers, especially those with families. Also, post-World War I budget reductions and the Great Depression led to irregularities in pay: often the soldier received only half his pay, or half his pay in money and half in consumer goods or food.

1-24. The rapid pace and acceptance of technology during the late 1930s caused the Army to create special "technician" ranks in grades 3, 4, & 5 (CPL, SGT & SSG), with chevrons marked with a "T." This led to an increase in promotions among technical personnel. The technician ranks ended in 1948, but they later reappeared as 'specialists' in 1955.

1-25. The typical First Sergeant of this period carried his administrative files in his pocket—a black book. The book contained the names of everyone in the company and their professional history (AWOLs, work habits, promotions, etc.). The book passed from first sergeant to first sergeant, staying within the company and providing the unit with a historical document. The first sergeant accompanied men on runs, the drill field, training, or the firing range. He was always at the forefront of everything the company did.

FM 7-22.7

World War 2

1-26. With the attack on Pearl Harbor in December 1941, the United States found itself in another major war. Mobilization greatly increased the numbers of Army noncommissioned officers. Ironically, mobilization, combined with other factors, created a staggering growth in the percentage of noncommissioned officers to total forces. The proportion of noncommissioned officers in the Army increased from 20 percent of the enlisted ranks in 1941, to nearly 50 percent in 1945, resulting in reduced prestige for many noncommissioned officer ranks. Coupled with this growth in numbers the eight-man infantry squad increased to twelve, with the sergeant then staff sergeant, replacing the corporal as its leader. The rank of corporal came to mean very little, even though he was in theory and by tradition a combat leader.

> **Staff Sergeant Kazuo Otani at Pieve Di St. Luce**
>
> World War II witnessed a number of heroic deeds by NCOs. An example was the action of Staff Sergeant Kazuo Otani on 15 July 1944, near Pieve Di St. Luce, Italy. Advancing to attack a hill objective, Staff Sergeant Otani's platoon became pinned down in a wheat field by concentrated fire from enemy machine gun and sniper positions. Realizing the danger confronting his platoon, Staff Sergeant Otani left his cover and shot and killed a sniper who was firing with deadly effect upon the platoon. Followed by a steady stream of machine gun bullets, Staff Sergeant Otani then dashed across the open wheat field toward the foot of a cliff, and directed his men to crawl to the cover of the cliff.
>
> When the movement of the platoon drew heavy enemy fire, he dashed along the cliff toward the left flank, exposing himself to enemy fire. By attracting the attention of the enemy, he enabled the men closest to the cliff to reach cover. Organizing these men to guard against possible enemy counterattack, Staff Sergeant Otani again made his way across the open field, shouting instructions to the stranded men while continuing to draw enemy fire. Reaching the rear of the platoon position, he took partial cover in a shallow ditch and directed covering fire for the men who had begun to move forward. At this point, one of his men became seriously wounded. Ordering his men to remain under cover, Staff Sergeant Otani crawled to the wounded soldier who was lying on open ground in full view of the enemy. Dragging the wounded soldier to a shallow ditch, Staff Sergeant Otani proceeded to render first aid treatment, but was mortally wounded by machine gun fire.

1-27. Basic training in World War II focused on hands-on experience instead of the classroom. NCOs conducted all training for soldiers. After basic training, a soldier went to his unit where his individual training continued. The major problem was that the rapid expansion of the Army had led to a proportionate decrease in experienced men in the noncommissioned officer

History and Background

ranks. Making this condition worse was the practice of quickly advancing in rank soldiers who showed potential while combat losses reduced the number of experienced NCOs.

1-28. Fighting in the Pacific and Europe required large numbers of men. Millions of men enlisted and America drafted millions more. Still the Army suffered from manpower shortages. In 1942 the Army formally added women to its ranks. By 1945 over 90,000 women had enlisted in the Army. Women served in administrative, technical, motor vehicle, food, supply, communications, mechanical and electrical positions during the war. After the war women continued to serve in a variety of roles in the Army. As a result of the continued growth of technology, a new emphasis on education began in the post-World War II era. This emphasis encouraged the young soldier to become better educated in order to advance in rank.

> **Staff Sergeant John Sjogren at San Jose Hacienda**
>
> On 23 May 1945, Company I, 160th Infantry was conducting an attack near San Jose Hacienda in the Philippine Islands. The attack was against a high precipitous ridge defended by a company of enemy riflemen, who were entrenched in spider holes and supported by well-sealed pillboxes housing automatic weapons with interlocking bands of fire. The terrain was such that only 1 squad could advance at one time; and from a knoll atop a ridge a pillbox covered the only approach with automatic fire. Against this enemy stronghold, Staff Sergeant John C. Sjogren led the first squad to open the assault. Deploying his men, he moved forward and was hurling grenades when he saw that his next in command, at the opposite flank, was gravely wounded. Without hesitation he crossed 20 yards of exposed terrain in the face of enemy fire and exploding dynamite charges, moved the man to cover and administered first aid.
>
> He then worked his way forward, advancing directly into the enemy fire, and killed 8 enemy soldiers in spider holes guarding the approach to the pillbox. Crawling to within a few feet of the pillbox while his men concentrated their bullets on the fire port, he began dropping grenades through the narrow firing slit. The enemy immediately threw these unexploded grenades out, and fragments from one wounded him in the hand and back. However, by hurling grenades through the embrasure faster then the enemy could return them, he succeeded in destroying the occupants. Despite his wounds, he directed his squad to follow him in a systematic attack on the remaining positions, which he eliminated in like manner, taking tremendous risks, overcoming bitter resistance, and never hesitating in his relentless advance. Staff Sergeant Sjogren led his squad in destroying 9 pillboxes, thereby paving the way for his company's successful advance.

FM 7-22.7

NCO Education I

1-29. On 30 June 1947 the first class enrolled in the 2d Constabulary Brigade's NCO school, located in Munich, Germany. Two years later, the US Seventh Army took over the 2d Constabulary functions and the school became the Seventh Army Noncommissioned Officers Academy. Eight years later AR 350-90 established Army-wide standards for NCO academies. Emphasis on NCO education increased to the point that by 1959 over 180,000 soldiers would attend NCO academies located in the continental United States. In addition to NCO academies, the Army encouraged enlisted men to advance their education by other means. By 1952 the Army had developed the Army Education Program to allow soldiers to attain credits for academic education. This program provided a number of ways for the enlisted man to attain a high school or college diploma.

Korea

1-30. In 1950 an unprepared United States again had to commit large numbers of troops in a war a half a world away. The North Korean attack on South Korea stressed American responsibilities overseas. Containment of communist aggression was the official policy of the United States. This meant that American commitments in Asia, Europe and the Pacific would require a strong and combat-ready professional Army. During the Korean War the NCO emerged more prominently as a battle leader than he had in World War II. The steep hills, ridges, narrow valleys and deep gorges forced many units to advance as squads. Korea was the first war America fought with an integrated Army. Black and white soldiers together fought a common foe.

Sergeant Ola Mize at Outpost Harry

Near Surang-ni, Sergeant Ola L. Mize led the defense of Outpost Harry. Learning of a wounded soldier in an outlying listening post, during an artillery barrage, Mize moved to rescue the soldier. Returning to the main position with the soldier, Mize rallied the troops into an effective defense as the enemy attacked in force. Knocked down three times with grenade or artillery blasts, Mize continued to lead his men.

With the enemy assault temporarily halted, Mize and several men moved from bunker to bunker clearing the enemy. Upon noticing a friendly machine gun position being overrun, he fought his way to their aid, killing ten enemy soldiers and dispersing the rest. Securing a radio, he directed artillery fire upon the enemy's approach routes. At dawn, Mize formed the survivors into a unit and successfully led a counterattack that cleared the enemy from the outpost.

1-31. In 1958 the Army added two grades to the NCO ranks. These pay grades, E-8 and E-9, would "provide for a better delineation of responsibilities in the enlisted structure." With the addition of these grades, the ranks of the

_____ **History and Background**

NCO were corporal, sergeant, staff sergeant, sergeant first class, master sergeant and sergeant major.

Vietnam

1-32. America's strategy of containment continued after the Korean War and the Nation set a course to help its ally South Vietnam defeat communist aggression. In 1965 America made a major commitment in ground troops to Vietnam. The Vietnamese Communists fought a long drawn-out war, meant to wear down American forces. Because no clear battle lines existed it was often hard to tell foe from friend. In 1973 a formal cease-fire signed by American and North Vietnamese delegations ended American troop commitments to the area.

1-33. Vietnam proved to be a junior leader's war with decentralized control. Much of the burden of combat leadership fell on the NCO. With a need for large numbers of NCOs for combat duty, the Army began the Noncommissioned Officer Candidate Course, with three sites at Fort Benning, Fort Knox and Fort Sill. After a 12-week course, the graduate became an E-5; those in the top five percent became E-6s. An additional 10 weeks of hands-on training followed and then the NCO went to Vietnam. However, senior NCOs had mixed feelings about the program (sometimes called the "shake-and-bake" program). Many of these senior NCOs thought it undermined the prestige of the NCO Corps though few could say they actually knew an unqualified NCO from the course.

> **SFC Eugene Ashley at Lang Vei**
>
> During the initial stages of the defense of the Special Forces camp at Lang Vei, Republic of Vietnam, SFC Eugene Ashley, Jr. supported the camp with high explosives and illumination mortar rounds. Upon losing communication with the camp, he directed air strikes and artillery support. He then organized a small assault force composed of local friendly forces.
>
> Five times Ashley and his newly formed unit attacked enemy positions, clearing the enemy and proceeding through booby-trapped bunkers. Wounded by machine gun fire, Ashley continued on, finally directing air strikes on his own position to clear the enemy. As the enemy retreated he lapsed into unconsciousness. While being transported down the hill, an enemy artillery shell fatally wounded him.

Sergeant Major of the Army

1-33. In 1966 Army Chief of Staff Harold K. Johnson chose Sergeant Major William O. Wooldridge as the first Sergeant Major of the Army. The SMA was to be the primary advisor and consultant to the Chief of Staff on enlisted matters. He would identify problems affecting enlisted personnel and recommend appropriate solutions.

FM 7-22.7

> *In his brief instructions, Johnson included on a 3 x 5 card that he presented to Wooldridge that he was to advise the Chief of Staff on 'all matters pertaining primarily to enlisted personnel, including ... morale, welfare, training, clothing, insignia, equipment, pay and allowances, customs and courtesies of the service, enlistment and reenlistment, discipline and promotion policies.'*
>
> *Wooldridge kept the folded card in his wallet, the only written instructions he had during his time in office. In a handwritten note to Wooldridge later Johnson stated 'You have shouldered a large burden and I am most appreciative of the way you have done it.'*
>
> *Since the establishment of the position of Sergeant Major of the Army, they have been working to refine and bring back professionalism to the NCO Corps and refining the focus of the Office of the Sergeant Major of the Army.*
>
> *Today's soldier can clearly identify with the top enlisted soldier serving at the head of the noncommissioned officer support channel and we owe a debt of gratitude to General Johnson and the men who have made it possible ... the Sergeants Major of the Army.*

POST-VIETNAM AND THE VOLUNTEER ARMY

NCO Education II

1-34. After the US ended conscription following the Vietnam War, it became increasingly clear NCOs needed more sustained training throughout their careers. NCO education expanded and became formalized in the 70s and 80s. Today's NCO Education System includes the Primary Leadership Development Course (PLDC), Basic Noncommissioned Officer Course (BNCOC), the Advanced Noncommissioned Officer Course (ANCOC), and the US Army Sergeants Major Course (USASMC). The Sergeants Major Course first began in January 1973 as the capstone training for the Army's most senior NCOs. The Sergeants Major Academy also operates three senior NCO courses outside NCOES that are designed to train NCOs for particular positions. These are the First Sergeant Course (FSC), the Battle Staff Course (BSC) and the Command Sergeant Major Course (CSMC). In 1986 PLDC became a mandatory prerequisite for promotion to staff sergeant. This was the first time an NCOES course actually became mandatory for promotion.

1-35. In 1987 the Army completed work on a new state-of-the-art education facility at the Sergeants Major Academy at Fort Bliss, Texas, further emphasizing the importance of professional education for NCOs. This 17.5 million-dollar, 125,000 square foot structure allowed the academy to expand course loads and number of courses. As the Noncommissioned Officer Education System continues to grow, the NCO of today combines history and tradition with skill and ability to prepare for combat. He retains the duties and responsibilities given to him by von Steuben in 1778 and these have been built upon to produce the soldier of today.

History and Background

Grenada and Panama

1-36. The murder of Grenada's Prime Minister in October 1983 created a breakdown in civil order that threatened the lives of American medical students living on the island. At the request of allied Caribbean nations, the United States invaded the island to safeguard the Americans there. Operation Urgent Fury included Army Rangers and Paratroopers from the 82nd Airborne Division. This action succeeded in the eventual reestablishment of a representative form of government in Grenada. After Manuel Noriega seized control of his country in 1983, corruption in the Panamanian government became widespread and eventually Noriega threatened the security of the United States by cooperating with Colombian drug producers. Harassment of American personnel increased and after a US Marine was shot in December 1989, the US launched Operation Just Cause. This invasion, including over 25,000 soldiers, quickly secured its objectives. Noriega surrendered on 3 January 1990 and was later convicted on drug trafficking charges.

The Gulf War

1-37. In August 1990 Iraqi military forces invaded and occupied Kuwait. The US immediately condemned Iraq's actions and began building support for a coalition to liberate Kuwait. Iraq's dictator, Saddam Hussein, ignored the demands of over 36 nations to leave Kuwait. In response, coalition forces began deploying to Saudi Arabia. On 12 January 1991 Congress authorized the use of military force to liberate Kuwait. Operation Desert Storm commenced 17 January 1991 as the coalition initiated an air campaign to disable Iraq's infrastructure. After five weeks of air and missile attacks, ground troops, including over 300,000 from the US Army, began their campaign to free Kuwait. On 27 February 1991, coalition forces entered Kuwait City forcing Iraq to concede a cease-fire after only 100 hours of ground combat.

Somalia and Rwanda

1-38. In the early 1990s Somalia was in the worst drought in over a century and its people were starving. The international community responded with humanitarian aid but clan violence threatened international relief efforts. The United Nations formed a US-led coalition to protect relief workers so aid could continue to flow into the country. Operation Restore Hope succeeded, ending the starvation of the Somali people. US soldiers also assisted in civic projects that built and repaired roads, schools, hospitals and orphanages. A history of ethnic hatred in Rwanda led to murder on a genocidal scale. Up to a million Rwandans were killed and two million Rwandans fled and settled in refugee camps in several central African locations. Conditions in the camps were appalling; starvation and disease took even more lives. The international community responded with one of the largest humanitarian relief efforts ever mounted. The US military quickly established an atmosphere of collaboration and coordination setting up the necessary infrastructure to complement and support the humanitarian response community. In Operation Support Hope, US Army soldiers provided clean water, assisted in burying the dead and integrated the transportation and distribution of relief supplies.

> **MSG Gordon and SFC Shughart at Mogadishu**
>
> On 17 October 1993, while serving as a Sniper Team with Task Force Ranger in Mogadishu, Somalia, Master Sergeant Gary I. Gordon and Sergeant First Class Randall D. Shughart provided precision sniper fires from the lead helicopter during an assault on a building and at two helicopter crash sites.
>
> While providing critical suppressive fires at the second crash site, MSG Gordon and SFC Shughart learned that ground forces were not immediately available to secure the site. They both unhesitatingly volunteered to be inserted to protect the four critically wounded personnel, despite being well aware of the growing number of enemy personnel closing in on the site.
>
> Equipped with only sniper rifles and pistols, MSG Gordon and SFC Shughart, while under intense small arms fire from the enemy, fought their way through a dense maze of shanties and shacks to reach the critically injured crewmembers. They immediately pulled the pilot and the other crewmembers from the aircraft, establishing a perimeter that placed themselves in the most vulnerable position. MSG Gordon and SFC Shughart used their long-range rifles and side arms to kill an undetermined number of attackers. Master Sergeant Gordon then went back to the wreckage, recovering some of the crew's weapons and ammunition. Despite the fact that he was critically low on ammunition, he provided some of it to the dazed pilot and then radioed for help. MSG Gordon and SFC Shughart continued to travel the perimeter, protecting the downed crew.
>
> SFC Shughart continued his protective fire until he depleted his ammunition and was fatally wounded. After he exhausted his own rifle ammunition, MSG Gordon returned to the wreckage, recovering a rifle with the last five rounds of ammunition and gave it to the pilot with the words, "good luck." Then, armed only with his pistol, MSG Gordon continued to fight until he was fatally wounded. The actions of MSG Gordon and SFC Shughart saved the pilot's life.

Haiti

1-39. In December 1990 Jean-Bertrand Aristide was elected President of Haiti, in an election that international observers deemed largely free and fair. Aristide took office in February 1991, but was overthrown by the Army and forced to leave the country. The human rights climate deteriorated as the military and the de facto government sanctioned atrocities in defiance of the international community's condemnation. The United States led a Multinational Force to restore democracy by removing the military regime, return the previously elected Aristide regime to power, ensure security, assist

_____ **History and Background**

with the rehabilitation of civil administration, train a police force, help prepare for elections and turn over responsibility to the UN. Operation Uphold Democracy succeeded both in restoring the democratically elected government of Haiti and in stemming emigration. In March 1995 the United States transferred the peacekeeping responsibilities to the United Nations.

The Balkans

1-40. During the mid-1990s, Yugoslavia was in a state of unrest because various ethnic groups wanted a separate state for themselves. Serbia attempted through military force to prevent any group from gaining autonomy from the central government. Serbian forces brutally suppressed the separatist movement of ethnic Albanians in the province of Kosovo, leaving hundreds dead and over 200,000 homeless. The refusal of Serbia to negotiate peace and strong evidence of mass murder by Serbian forces resulted in the commencement of Operation Allied Force. Air strikes against Serbian military targets continued for 78 days in an effort to bring an end to the atrocities that continued to be waged by the Serbs. Serbian forces withdrew and NATO deployed a peacekeeping force, including US Army soldiers, to restore stability to the region and assist in the repair of the civilian infrastructure.

> **SGT Christine Roberts in Kosovo**
>
> In June 1999, SGT Christine Roberts was a flight medic with the 50th Medical Company at Camp Bondsteel in Kosovo. Her air ambulance crew was called to assist when a soldier lost his right foot after he stepped on a land mine while on patrol near Basici, Kosovo. Roberts rode a jungle-penetrator 200 feet down onto the steep hill to search by foot, disregarding the potential danger from other mines. After finding the casualty, she dressed his injured leg, tightened a tourniquet and then loaded him on the hoist. He was lifted out from the wooded, mountainous terrain into the helicopter and flown to the hospital at Camp Bondsteel. SGT Roberts received the Soldier's Medal for her heroism.

The War on Terrorism

1-41. Terrorists of the al-Qaeda network attacked the United States on September 11, 2001, killing nearly 3000 people and destroying the World Trade Center in New York City. The United States, with enormous support from the global community, responded with attacks on the al-Qaeda network and the Taliban-controlled government of Afghanistan that was providing it support. Operation Enduring Freedom with US and allied forces quickly toppled the Taliban regime and severely damaged the al-Qaeda forces in Afghanistan. US Army NCOs and soldiers continue to play a leading role in the war on terrorism and provide security to the Nation.

CONTEMPORARY OPERATIONAL ENVIRONMENT

Full Spectrum Operations

1-42. Today the Army's operational doctrine covers the full spectrum of operations. That means stability, support, offense and defense operations. What that means to you is to conduct good training and make sure your soldier meets the standards. Effective training is the cornerstone of operational success. Training to high standards is essential for a full spectrum force; the Army cannot predict every operation it deploys to. Battle-focused training on combat tasks prepares soldiers, units and leaders to deploy, fight and win. Upon alert, initial-entry Army forces deploy immediately, conduct operations and complete any needed mission-specific training in country. Follow-on forces conduct pre- or post-deployment mission rehearsal exercises, abbreviated if necessary, based on available time and resources.

The Operational Environment

1-43. America's potential adversaries learned from the Gulf War that to oppose US forces on our terms is foolhardy at best and may even be suicidal. As demonstrated by terrorist adversaries, we can expect that our enemies in the future will attempt to avoid decisive battle; prolong the conflict; conduct sophisticated ambushes; disperse combat forces and attempt to use information

History and Background

services to its advantage — all while inflicting unacceptable casualties on US forces.

1-44. The operational environment and the wide array of threats present significant challenges. Army forces must simultaneously defeat an adversary while protecting noncombatants and the infrastructure on which they depend. This requires Army leaders to be adaptive and aware of their environment.

> *"Large units are likely to conduct simultaneous offensive, defensive, stability and support operations. Units at progressively lower echelons receive missions that require fewer combinations. At lower echelons, units usually perform only one type of operation."*
>
> FM 3-0, *Operations*, 2001

1-45. Depending on your mission and location, you and your soldiers, or perhaps the local population may be the targets of a terrorist attack. An adversary may try to use you in an information campaign to destroy US resolve. The more vital your units' mission is to the overall operation the more likely it is that an adversary will attempt to target you in some way.

The Information Environment

1-46. All military operations take place within an information environment that is not within the control of military forces. The information environment is the combination of individuals, organizations and systems that collect, process, store, display and disseminate information. It also includes the information itself. The media's use of real-time technology affects public opinion and may alter the conduct of military operations. Now, more than ever, every soldier represents America — potentially to a global audience.

1-47. Technology enhances leader, unit and soldier performance and affects how Army forces conduct full spectrum operations in peace, conflict and war. Even with its advantages, the side with superior technology does not always win in land operations; rather, the side that applies combat power more skillfully usually prevails. The skill of soldiers coupled with the effectiveness of leaders decides the outcomes of engagements, battles and campaigns.

ARMY TRANSFORMATION

1-48. The NCO has a key role in Army Transformation, perhaps the premier role. As the Army becomes a more deployable, agile and responsive force, some units will reorganize, receive new equipment and learn new tactics. The NCO, as the leader most responsible for individual and small unit training, will build the foundation for the Army's objective force. New technology enables you to cover more ground and maintain better situational awareness. But individual and collective tasks are more complex, requiring small unit leaders

FM 7-22.7 _____

to coordinate and synchronize soldiers' efforts and the systems they employ to a degree never before seen.

> *"One thing some soldiers may not fully understand yet is that transformation involves a lot more than two brigades up at Fort Lewis - it's about the future and what kind of Army we'll have for decades to come. We will continue to man, modernize and train our current forces throughout the transformation.... We will continue to need sharp, quick-thinking leaders. The variety of missions and volume of information they'll be given will place a lot of responsibility on them.*
>
> *"Transformation could cause as many changes in training and developing leaders in our schools as tactics and equipment. The result will be a future that lets us put a more powerful force on the ground faster and that will save a lot of lives. These are interesting times and sergeants need to stay open minded, keep updated on transformation and be thinking about how it will impact the NCO Corps."*
>
> SMA Jack L. Tilley

1-49. Our Army has always benefited from NCOs who could and did display initiative, make decisions and seize opportunities that corresponded with the commander's intent. These qualities are more important than ever in Army Transformation. Despite technological improvement and increased situational awareness at every level – the small unit leader must still make decisions that take advantage of fleeting opportunities on the battlefield.

> *"The great strength about the Army is: we're adaptable. Given the right tools [soldiers] make it hum."*
>
> GEN John N. Abrams

ARMY VALUES

1-50. You know what the Army Values are. They are important because they define character traits that help develop and maintain discipline. These values and the resulting discipline cause soldiers to do the right thing and continue doing the right thing even when it is hard. In leaders these traits are doubly important – we all know that actions speak louder than words. Your soldiers watch what you do as well as listen to what you say. You can't just carry values around on your keychain – demonstrate them in all you do.

LOYALTY

Bear true faith and allegiance to the US Constitution, the Army, your unit and other soldiers.

1-51. Stand by your soldiers' honest mistakes – they can't learn without making a few. Take pride in their accomplishments and ensure your superiors hear about them. Make sure they understand their mission, know how to accomplish it and why it is important. Know that you and your soldiers are part of a bigger picture and every soldier has a task that supports the overall objective. When the commander makes a decision, execute – don't talk down about it either with your peers or your soldiers.

> *"Loyalty is the big thing, the greatest battle asset of all. But no one ever wins the loyalty of troops by preaching loyalty. It is given to him as he proves his possession of the other virtues."*
>
> BG S. L. A. Marshall

DUTY

Fulfill your obligations.

1-52. Take responsibility and do what's right, no matter how tough it is, even when no one is watching. Accomplish all assigned or implied tasks to the fullest of your ability. Duty requires a willingness to accept full responsibility for your actions and for your soldiers' performance. Take the initiative and anticipate requirements based on the situation. You will be asked to put the Nation's welfare and mission accomplishment ahead of the personal safety of you and your soldiers.

> *"The essence of duty is acting in the absence of orders or direction from others, based on an inner sense of what is morally and professionally right...."*
>
> GEN John A. Wickham Jr.

RESPECT

Treat people as they should be treated.

1-53. Respect is treating others with consideration and honor. It is the expectation that others are as committed to getting the job done as you are while accepting they may have different ways of doing so. You don't have to accept every suggestion to show respect; just expect honesty and professionalism. Conduct corrective training with the end in mind — to help that soldier develop discipline and ultimately survive on the battlefield.

> *"Regardless of age or grade, soldiers should be treated as mature individuals. They are engaged in an honorable profession and deserve to be treated as such."*
>
> GEN Bruce Clarke

FM 7-22.7

SELFLESS SERVICE

Put the welfare of the Nation, the Army and your soldiers before your own.

1-54. What is best for our Nation, Army and organization must always come first. Selfless service is placing your duty before your personal desires. It is the ability to endure hardships and insurmountable odds in the service of fellow soldiers and our country. Placing your duty and your soldiers' welfare before your personal desires has always been key to the uniqueness of the American NCO.

"The Nation today needs soldiers who think in terms of service to their country and not in terms of their country's debt to them."

General of the Army Omar N. Bradley

HONOR

Live up to all the Army values.

1-55. Honor is living up to the Army Values. It starts with being honest with one's self and being truthful and sincere in all of our actions. As GEN Douglas MacArthur once said, "The untruthful soldier trifles with the lives of his countrymen and the honor and safety of his country." Being honest with one's self is perhaps the best way to live the Army Values. If something does not seem right to you or someone asks you to compromise your values, then you need to assess the situation and take steps to correct or report the issue.

"What is life without honor? Degradation is worse than death."

Lieutenant General Thomas J. "Stonewall" Jackson

INTEGRITY

Do what's right, legally and morally.

1-56. Integrity obliges one to act when duty calls. Integrity means to firmly adhere to a code of moral and ethical principles. Living and speaking with integrity is very hard. You must live by your word for everything, no buts, no excuses. Having integrity and being honest in everything you say and do builds trust. As leaders, all soldiers are watching and looking to see that you are honest and live by your word. If you make a mistake, you should openly acknowledge it, learn from it and move forward.

"The American people rightly look to their military leaders not only to be skilled in the technical aspects of the profession of arms, but also to be men of integrity."

GEN J. Lawton Collins

_____ **History and Background**

PERSONAL COURAGE
Face fear, danger, or adversity (Physical or Moral).

1-57. Persevere in what you know to be right and don't tolerate wrong behavior in others. Physical courage is overcoming fears of bodily harm while performing your duty. Moral courage is overcoming fears while doing what is right even if unpopular. It takes special courage to make and support unpopular decisions. Do not compromise your values or moral principles. If you believe you are right after thoughtful consideration, hold to your position. We expect and encourage candor and integrity from all soldiers. Taking the immediate and right actions in a time of conflict will save lives.

"The concept of professional courage does not always mean being as tough as nails either. It also suggests a willingness to listen to the soldiers' problems, to go to bat for them in a tough situation and it means knowing just how far they can go. It also means being willing to tell the boss when he's wrong."

SMA William Connelly

1-58. By accepting Army Values and by your example passing them on to your soldiers, you help develop and spread the warrior ethos throughout the Army. The warrior ethos is that frame of mind whereby soldiers will not quit until they have accomplished their mission. It "compels soldiers to fight through all conditions to victory, no matter how long it takes and no matter how much effort is required. It is the soldier's selfless commitment to the Nation, mission, unit and fellow soldiers. It is the professional attitude that inspires every American soldier. The warrior ethos is grounded in refusal to accept failure. It is developed and sustained through discipline, example, commitment to Army values and pride in the Army's heritage."

> **Corporal Rodolfo Hernandez on Hill 420**
>
> CPL Rodolfo P. Hernandez, G Company, 187th Regimental Combat Team was with his platoon on Hill 420 near Wontong-ni, Korea on May 31st, 1951. His platoon came under ruthless attack by a numerically superior and fanatical hostile force, accompanied by heavy artillery, mortar and machinegun fire that inflicted numerous casualties on the platoon. His comrades were forced to withdraw due to lack of ammunition but CPL Hernandez, although wounded in an exchange of grenades, continued to deliver deadly fire into the ranks of the onrushing assailants until a ruptured cartridge rendered his rifle inoperative. Immediately leaving his position, CPL. Hernandez rushed the enemy armed only with rifle and bayonet. Fearlessly engaging the foe, he killed 6 of the enemy before falling unconscious from grenade, bayonet and bullet wounds but his heroic action momentarily halted the enemy advance and enabled his unit to counterattack and retake the lost ground.

FM 7-22.7

NCO PROFESSIONAL DEVELOPMENT

1-59. The leader development process is executed in three pillars: Institutional Training, Operational Assignments and Self- Development. The Noncommissioned Officer Education System (NCOES) is the keystone for NCO development. NCOES provides leader and MOS skill training in an integrated system of resident training at four levels. This is a continuous cycle of education, training, experience, assessment, feedback and reinforcement. The needs of the unit and the demonstrated potential of the leaders are always kept in focus and balanced at all times. The emphasis is on developing competent and confident leaders who understand and are able to exploit the full potential of current and future Army doctrine. Self-development ties together NCOs' experience and training to make them better leaders, which ultimately benefit their units' combat readiness. See Figure 1-1.

Noncommissioned officers, properly to perform the duties of their position, require, and should receive, a special education

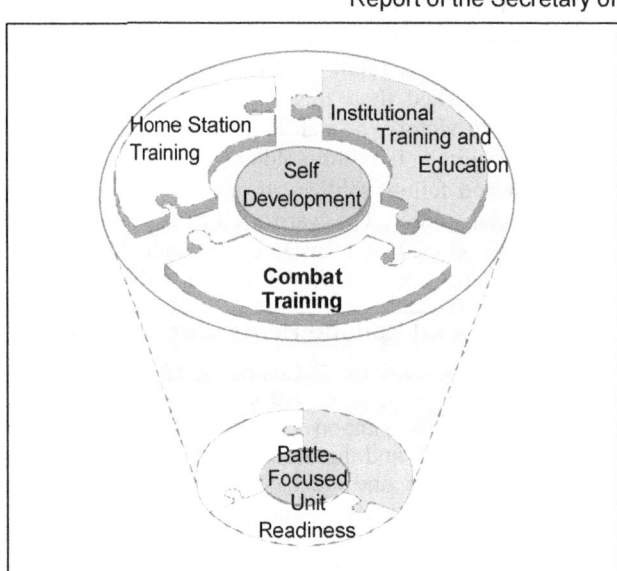

Report of the Secretary of War, 1888

Figure 1-1. Army Training and Education Program

The NCO Education System

1-60. PLDC: The first leadership course NCOs will likely attend is the non-MOS specific Primary Leadership Development Course (PLDC) conducted at sixteen Noncommissioned Officer Academies (NCOA) worldwide. Soldiers may appear before the promotion board and can be conditionally promoted to sergeant prior to attending PLDC. Commanders and First Sergeants should closely monitor the announced MOS cutoff scores in programming soldiers to attend PLDC.

> *"The purpose of the Noncommissioned Officer Education System is to build NCO trust and confidence, to raise tactical and technical competence and to inculcate the essential values of the professional Army ethic through the corps."*
>
> COL Kenneth Simpson and CSM Oren Bevins

1-61. BNCOC: Combat arms (CA) /combat support (CS) /combat service support (CSS) Basic NCO Course occurs at proponent service schools. Successful completion of BNCOC is a prerequisite for consideration for promotion to Sergeant First Class. Active component sergeants promotable to Staff Sergeant can be conditionally promoted prior to attendance at BNCOC, but must complete the course within one year. Reserve component sergeants must first complete Phase I. Training varies in length from two to nineteen weeks with an average of nine weeks. A 12-day common core, designed by the US Army Sergeants Major Academy, supplements leadership training received at PLDC. The Department of the Army funds all BNCOC courses. Priority for attendance is SSG and SGT (P).

1-62. The BNCOC Automated Reservation System (BARS) schedules Active Component soldiers to attend BNCOC while the Reserve Component uses ATRRS (Army Training and Requirements Resource System). The systems provide the Army Personnel Command (PERSCOM) with an order of merit listing of soldiers eligible to attend BNCOC. The order of merit listing is based on criteria established by the Office of the Deputy Chief of Staff for Personnel (ODCSPER) and the Office of the Deputy Chief of Staff for Operations (ODCSOPS). The report enables PERSCOM to identify the "best qualified" soldiers for training and nominates them to their commander for verification that the soldier is qualified to attend BNCOC. Commanders have the option of canceling the PERSCOM nomination if the soldier is unqualified. If the commander cancels the nomination, PERSCOM will then select a replacement from the Army wide order of merit list.

1-63. Department of the Army selects Advanced NCO Course (ANCOC) attendees by a centralized SFC promotion / Advanced Noncommissioned Officer Course Selection Board. The zone of consideration is announced by PERSCOM before each board convenes. SSGs (P) can be conditionally promoted prior to attending ANCOC but must complete the course within a year. SSGs (P) can be conditionally promoted prior to and during the course to sergeant first class. All soldiers selected for promotion to SFC who have not previously attended ANCOC are automatic selectees. Priority for ANCOC attendance is SFC and SSG (P).

FM 7-22.7

1-64. USASMC. The US Army Sergeants Major Course (USASMC) is the senior level NCOES course and the capstone of NCO education. The USASMC is a nine-month resident course conducted at Fort Bliss, TX. Selected individuals may complete USASMC through non-resident training. A Department of the Army centralized selection board determines who attends resident or non-resident training. Soldiers selected for promotion to SGM or appointment to CSM who are not graduates will attend the next resident USASMC. Soldiers may not decline once selected. USASMC is a requirement for promotion to SGM. MSGs (P) can be conditionally promoted to SGM prior to and during the course to sergeant major. NCOs who complete the Sergeants Major Course incur a two-year service obligation.

> *"... the program of instruction is very demanding, particularly in the areas of human relations and military organization and operations."*
>
> MSG Henry Caro, regarding the Sergeants Major Course

Operational Assignments

1-65. Operational experience provides leaders the opportunity to use and build upon what was learned through the process of formal education. Experience gained through a variety of challenging duty assignments prepares NCOs to lead soldiers in combat. An NCO's MOS is usually the basis for operational assignments. Special duty assignments present unique opportunities for leader development as the NCO is often performing duties outside his or her PMOS (e.g. drill instructor, recruiting, joint duty and NCOES Instructor). Commanders and leaders use the unit Leader Development Program (LDP) and NCO Development Program to enhance NCO development during operational assignments.

1-66. Developing leaders is a priority mission in command and organizations. Commanders, leaders and supervisors develop soldiers and ensure necessary educational requirements are met. Commanders establish formal unit LDPs that focus on developing individual leaders. These programs normally consist of three phases: reception and integration, basic skill development, and advanced development and sustainment.

- Reception and Integration. The 1SG and CSM interview new NCOs and discuss the new leader's duty position, previous experience and training, personal goals and possible future assignments. Some units may administer a diagnostic test to identify strengths and weaknesses. The 1SG and CSM use this information to help design a formal developmental program specific to that new leader.
- Basic Skill Development. The new leader attains a minimum acceptable level of proficiency in critical tasks necessary to perform his mission. The responsibility for this phase lies with the new NCOs immediate supervisor, assisted by other key NCOs and officers.

History and Background

- Advanced Development and Sustainment. This phase sustains proficiency in tasks already mastered and develops new skills. This is often done through additional duty assignments, technical or developmental courses and self-development.

NCODP

1-67. The NCO Development Program (NCODP) is the CSM's leader development program for NCOs. NCODP encompasses most training at the unit level and is tailored to the unique requirements of the unit and its NCOs. NCODP should be 75% METL-driven tasks and 25% general military subjects such as Customs, Courtesies and Traditions of the US Army.

> *You must learn more so that you can do more for your [soldiers] as well as prepare for higher rank and greater responsibility.*
>
> The Noncom's Guide, 1948

Self-development

1-68. Self-development is a life-long, standards-based, competency driven process that is progressive and sequential and complements institutional and operational experiences to provide personal and professional development. It is accomplished through structured and non-structured, technical and academic learning experiences conducted in multiple environments using traditional, technology-enhanced and self-directed methods. Self-development consists of individual study, education, research, professional reading, practice and self-assessment.

> *"A sergeant can't say on the one hand, 'self-improvement is essential,' then on the other hand put off Army schooling or other self-development programs."*
>
> CSM George D. Mock and SFC John K. D'Amato

1-69. Self-development includes both structured and self-motivated development tasks. At junior levels, self-development is very structured and narrowly focused. It is tailored towards building the basic leader skills and closely tied with unit NCO Development Programs. The components may be distance learning, directed reading programs or other activities that directly relate to building direct leader skills. As NCOs become more senior in rank, self-motivated development becomes more important – activities like professional reading or college courses that help the senior NCO develop organizational leadership skills.

1-70. **Professional Development Models (PDM).** PDMs are available for each Career Management Field. You can find these in DA PAM 600-25 "The US Army Noncommissioned Officer Professional Development Guide."

FM 7-22.7

PDMs provide both career and educational 'road maps' for NCOs to assist in self-development.

- Portray institutional training and operational assignments in relation to CMF recommended self-development activities. Leader self-development is an individual soldier responsibility over which a soldier has direct control.
- Emphasize self-development. Soldiers should not over-emphasize educational activities to the point where self-development takes precedence over duty performance.
- List operational assignments as examples of a career path. Soldiers should consult with their supervisors for their particular CMF progression.
- Guide soldiers through CMF proponent recommended activities to become more proficient at current and next higher missions.
- Complement and supplement NCOES institution instruction and Skill Level experiences without duplicating them.
- Focus on broad, general recommendations that address skills, knowledge and attitudes successful NCOs have found to be beneficial to their career progression. Each PDM lists recommended self-development activities to accomplish prior to NCOES courses and during specific MOS skill levels.
- Recommend goals to include professional certification and degrees related to the soldier's CMF. There are alternate methods of achieving recommendations, e.g., examinations, correspondence courses, learning center activities and education counselors that can assist soldiers in finding appropriate activities.
- Offer a series of planned, progressive, sequential developmental activities that leaders can follow to enhance and sustain military leadership competencies throughout their careers. Self-development activities require sacrifice of off-duty time to achieve desired goals.
- Provide the recommended activities soldiers can take to better prepare themselves for each phase of NCOES and to perform in each duty assignment.
- Review branch guidance on the appropriate PERSCOM branch website.

1-71. Educational Activities in Support of Self-Development.
Self-development activities recommended in PDMs draw on the programs and services offered through the Army Continuing Education System (ACES) which operate education centers throughout the Army.

- E-learning through Army Knowledge Online (AKO). AKO has or can direct an NCO to various college courses and other learning activities that directly support the NCO's MOS and self-development goals. Through your Army Knowledge Online account complete an ATRRS (Army Training Requirements and Resource System) application.
- Education Center Counseling Service. Academic and vocational counseling services to assist soldiers establishing professional and educational goals.

History and Background

- Functional Academic Skills Training. Instruction in reading, mathematics and communication skills to prepare for advanced training and meet prerequisites for further education. These courses can help soldiers achieve the recommended reading grade level (10 - PLDC, 11 - BNCOC and ANCOC and 12 –SMC). This is an on-duty commander's program to ensure soldiers possess the necessary reading and writing skills to succeed.

- High School Completion. This is an off-duty program to help soldiers earn a high school diploma or equivalency certificate.

- College Courses. Each installation education center arranges with colleges to provide courses on post that lead to a degree. Tuition Assistance (TA) is authorized to pay for voluntary off-duty educational programs that support the educational objectives of the Army and the soldier's self-development goals. This program helps soldiers earn associate, baccalaureate and graduate degrees.

- Testing. Education centers offer a wide range of academic and vocational interest tests. Some of the tests available are the Test of Adult Basic Education (TABE); Reading Comprehension Test for NCOES; Scholastic Assessment Test (SAT) and American College Test (ACT) for college entrance; and CLEP tests for college credit.

- Language Training. For non-linguists, ACES provides host-nation orientation and instruction in basic language skills. These courses enhance language skills of soldiers whose primary duties require frequent contact with host-nation counterparts. Materials are also available for sustainment of language skills.

- Correspondence Courses. The Defense Activity for Non-Traditional Education Support (DANTES) publishes a catalog of post-secondary correspondence courses soldiers can enroll in as an alternative to attending regular classroom courses. TA is available for approved courses. Educational counselors can advise soldiers.

- Army Learning Centers. These centers support self-development, unit and individual training. They provide a variety of independent study materials, computer based instruction, language labs, tutorial services and a military publications library.

- Army Correspondence Course Programs (ACCP). The ACCP provides a variety of self-study correspondence courses specific to Career Management Fields (CMF) and Military Occupational Specialties (MOS). Courses are also available in leadership and training management. Each course and sub-course earns soldiers promotion points upon successful completion. Enroll at the unit or the learning center.

FM 7-22.7

THE NCO TRANSITION

Today you have started a new chapter in your career in the Army. You are now a part of the noncommissioned officer corps in the profession of arms. The transition from an enlisted soldier to a noncommissioned officer is a historical tradition that can be traced to the Army of Frederick the Great.

The journey from junior enlisted to junior NCO is complex. You must now transition from one that was cared for to one who cares for others and from one who was taught to one that teaches, prepares for and supervises tasks. You might stay in the same section or perhaps you will move to a different organization entirely. Either way, you will do the job you have been trained to do – lead soldiers.

An NCO's job is not easy. You must speak with your own voice when giving orders - don't show favoritism. This is especially true for your former peers. You must treat each soldier the same and give him the respect he deserves, as you will expect to receive the same treatment in return. Remember that you are now responsible and accountable for your soldiers. The Army expects total commitment from those who are selected to lead, train and care for its soldiers.

Being an NCO is extremely rewarding. It is an honor and a privilege to lead America's finest men and women during peacetime and at war. Never forget this awesome responsibility.

Army values, the NCO Charge, the NCO Vision and the NCO Creed each provide guidance and inspiration to lead from the front. Live each and every day by the NCO Creed and include it in your daily business. The NCO Creed will help you through tough times and situations.

Chapter 2

Duties, Responsibilities and Authority of the NCO

Do the right thing – always

	Page
Assuming a Leadership Position	2-3
Duties, Responsibilities and Authority	2-4
Duty	2-4
Responsibility	2-5
Authority	2-7
Inspections and Corrections	2-10
Types of Inspections	2-11
Noncommissioned, Commissioned and Warrant Officer Relationships	2-14
The Commissioned Officer	2-14
The Warrant Officer	2-15
The Noncommissioned Officer	2-15
Special Mention	2-16
The Noncommissioned Officer Support Channel	2-17
NCO Ranks	2-19

FM 7-22.7

    Sergeant Major of the Army..2-19
    Command Sergeant Major and Sergeant Major....................2-19
    First Sergeant and Master Sergeant....................................2-21
    Platoon Sergeant and Sergeant First Class.........................2-21
    Squad, Section and Team Leaders......................................2-22
You Are a Noncommissioned Officer..2-23

For more information on Duties, Responsibilities and Authority of the NCO see AR 600-20, "Army Command Policy," DA PAM 600-25, "US Army NCO Professional Development Guide" and FM 6-22 (22-100), *Army Leadership.*

For more information on inspections see FM 22-5, *Drill and Ceremonies* **and AR 1-201, "Army Inspection Policy."**

_____ Duties, Responsibilities and Authority of the NCO

ASSUMING A LEADERSHIP POSITION

2-1. Assuming a leadership position is one of the most important leadership situations you'll face as an NCO. Everything discussed in FM 6-22 (22-100) about what you must **BE, KNOW and DO** is relevant to your success of assuming a leadership position.

2-2. When assuming a leadership position, there are some things to think about and learn as you establish your goals in the organization. Figure 2-1 will assist you in achieving your goals.

- Determine what your organization expects of you.
- Determine who your immediate leader is and what they expect of you.
- Determine the level of competence and the strengths and weaknesses of your soldiers.
- Identify the key people outside of your organization whose willing support you need to accomplish the mission.

Figure 2-1. Tasks to Assume a Leadership Position

2-3. You should also talk to your leaders, peers and key people such as the chaplain and the sergeant major. Seek clear answers to the questions in Figure 2-2.

- What is the organization's mission?
- How does this mission fit in with the mission of the next higher organization?
- What are the standards the organization must meet?
- What resources are available to help the organization accomplish the mission?
- What is the current state of morale?
- Who reports directly to you?
- What are the strengths and weaknesses of your key subordinates and the unit?
- Who are the key people outside the organization who support mission accomplishment? (What are their strengths and weaknesses?)
- When and what do you talk to your soldiers about?

Figure 2-2. Questions When Assuming a Leadership Position

2-4. Be sure to ask these questions at the right time, of the right person and in the best way. The answers to these questions and others you may have will help you to correctly assess the situation and select the right leadership style.

FM 7-22.7

DUTIES, RESPONSIBILITIES AND AUTHORITY

2-5. As a noncommissioned officer, you have duties, responsibilities and authority. Do you know the meaning of duties, responsibilities and authority?

DUTY

2-6. A duty is something you must do by virtue of your position and is a legal or moral obligation. For example, it is the supply sergeant's duty to issue equipment and keep records of the unit's supplies. It is the first sergeant's duty to hold formations, instruct platoon sergeants and assist the commander in supervising unit operations. It is the duty of the squad/section/team leader to account for his soldiers and ensure that they receive necessary instructions and are properly trained to perform their jobs.

2-7. A noncommissioned officer's duties are numerous and must be taken seriously. An NCO's duty includes taking care of soldiers, which is your priority. Corporals and sergeants do this by developing a genuine concern for their soldiers' well-being. Leaders must know and understand their soldiers well enough to train them as individuals and teams to operate proficiently. This will give them confidence in their ability to perform well under the difficult and demanding conditions of battle. Individual training is the principle duty and responsibility of NCOs. No one in the Army has more to do with training soldiers than NCOs. Well trained soldiers will likely succeed and survive on the battlefield. Well trained soldiers properly do the tasks their NCOs give them. A good leader executes the boss's decisions with energy and enthusiasm; looking at their leader, soldiers will believe the leader thinks it's absolutely the best possible solution.

> *"We don't need 'leaders' who stay warm on cold days... while their men freeze on the grenade ranges. If they get cold, the leader ought to get just as cold. And when he marches back to the barracks with them after that kind of day, they know he is one of them."*
>
> Drill Sergeant Karl Baccene

2-8. There may be situations you must think carefully about what you're told to do. For example, duty requires that you refuse to obey illegal orders. This is not a privilege you can claim, but a duty you must perform. You have no choice but to do what's ethically and legally correct. Making the right choice and acting on it when faced with an ethical question can be difficult. Sometimes, it means standing your ground and telling your supervisor you think their wrong. If you think an order is illegal, first be sure that you understand both the details of the order and its original intent. Seek clarification from the person who gave the order. This takes moral courage, but the question will be straightforward: Did you really mean for me to... steal the part... submit a false report... shoot the prisoners?

Duties, Responsibilities and Authority of the NCO

"Moral courage, to me, is much more demanding than physical courage."

SMA Leon L. Van Autreve

2-9. If the question is complex and time permits, seek advice from legal assistance. However, if you must decide immediately, as in the heat of combat, make the best judgment possible based on the Army values and attributes, your experience and your previous study and reflection. You take a risk when you disobey what you perceive to be an illegal order. Talk to your superiors, particularly those who have done what you aspire to do or what you think you'll be called on to do; providing counsel of this sort is an important part of leadership. Obviously, you need to make time to do this before you're faced with a tough call. This could possibly be the most difficult decision you'll ever make, but that's what leaders do.

2-10. Noncommissioned officers have three types of duties: specified duties, directed duties and implied duties.

2-11. **Specified duties** are those related to jobs and positions. Directives such as Army regulations, Department of the Army (DA) general orders, the Uniform Code of Military Justice (UCMJ), soldier's manuals, Army Training and Evaluation Program (ARTEP) publications and MOS job descriptions specify the duties. For example, AR 600-20 says that NCOs must ensure that their soldiers get proper individual training and maintain personal appearance and cleanliness.

2-12. **Directed duties** are not specified as part of a job position or MOS or other directive. A superior gives them orally or in writing. Directed duties include being in charge of quarters (CQ) or serving as sergeant of the guard, staff duty officer, company training NCO and NBC NCO, where these duties are not found in the unit's organization charts.

2-13. **Implied duties** often support specified duties, but in some cases they may not be related to the MOS job position. These duties may not be written but implied in the instructions. They're duties that improve the quality of the job and help keep the unit functioning at an optimum level. In most cases, these duties depend on individual initiative. They improve the work environment and motivate soldiers to perform because they want to, not because they have to. For example, while not specifically directed to do so, you hold in-ranks inspections daily to ensure your soldiers' appearance and equipment are up to standards.

RESPONSIBILITY

2-14. Responsibility is being accountable for what you do or fail to do. NCOs are responsible to fulfill not only their individual duties, but also to ensure their teams and units are successful. Any duty, because of the position you hold in the unit, includes a responsibility to execute that duty. As an NCO, you are accountable for your personal conduct and that of your soldiers. Also, each soldier is individually responsible for his own personal conduct and that responsibility cannot be delegated. A soldier is accountable for his actions to fellow soldiers, leaders, unit and the US Army.

2-15. As a leader you must ensure that your soldiers clearly understand their responsibilities as members of the team and as representative of the Army. Commanders set overall policies and standards, but all leaders must provide the guidance, resources, assistance and supervision necessary for soldiers to perform their duties. Mission accomplishment demands that officers and NCOs work together to advise, assist and learn from each other. Responsibilities fall into two categories: command and individual.

2-16. **Command responsibility** refers to collective or organizational accountability and includes how well the unit performs their missions. For example, a company commander is responsible for all the tasks and missions assigned to the company; his superiors hold him accountable for completing them. Commanders give military leaders the responsibility for what their sections, units, or organizations do or fail to do. NCOs are therefore responsible to fulfill not only their individual duties, but also to ensure that their team and unit are successful. The amount of responsibility delegated to you depends on your mission, the position you hold and your own willingness to accept responsibility.

2-17. One point you need to get straight is that although a list of duties can be drawn up describing what is expected of you, it will not tell you how to do your job. For example, one of an NCO's duties is to enforce standards of military appearance. This means you are responsible for correcting soldiers who wear the uniform improperly and for teaching them the correct standards of appearance. It also means that you should inspect for proper and serviceability, clothing and equipment of your soldiers. Remember that you must set the example first and your soldiers will follow in your footsteps.

> *"Rank is a badge of responsibility..."*
>
> DA Pam 360-1 (1957)

2-18. **Individual responsibility** as a noncommissioned officer means you are accountable for your personal conduct. Soldiers in the Army have their own responsibilities. For example, if you write a check at the commissary, it is your responsibility to have sufficient funds in the bank account to cover the check. Individual responsibility cannot be delegated; it belongs to the soldier that wrote the check. Soldiers are accountable for their actions, to their fellow

Duties, Responsibilities and Authority of the NCO

soldiers, to their leaders, to their unit and to the United States Army. As a leader you must ensure that your soldiers understand clearly their responsibilities as members of the team and as representatives of the Army.

> *"A leader does not 'choose' the best or most opportune time in which to lead. A good leader takes the challenge whenever and wherever it presents itself and does the best he or she can."*
>
> SMA Richard A. Kidd

AUTHORITY

2-19. As a noncommissioned officer, you must know what authority you have and where it comes from. You are also expected to use good judgment when exercising your authority.

2-20. Authority is defined as the right to direct soldiers to do certain things. Authority is the legitimate power of leaders to direct soldiers or to take action within the scope of their position. Military authority begins with the Constitution, which divides it between Congress and the President. The President, as commander in chief, commands the armed forces, including the Army. The authority from the Commander-in-Chief extends through the chain of command, with the assistance of the NCO support channel, to the squad, section or team leader who then directs and supervises the actions of individual soldiers. When you say, "PFC Lee, you and PFC Johnson start filling sandbags; SPC Garcia and SPC Smith will provide security from that hill," you are turning into action the orders of the entire chain of command.

2-21. In the Army there are two basic types of authority: command authority and general military authority.

2-22. **Command authority** is the authority leaders have over soldiers by virtue of rank or assignment. Command authority originates with the President and may be supplemented by law or regulation. Even though it is called "command" authority, it is not limited to officers – you have command authority inherent in your leadership position as a tank commander or team leader, for example. Noncommissioned officers' command authority is inherent with the job by virtue of position to direct or control soldiers.

> *"It takes guts for an NCO to use inherent authority and responsibility in training, maintaining, leading, and caring for soldiers."*
>
> SMA Glen E. Morrell

2-23. Leading soldiers includes the authority to organize, direct and control your assigned soldiers so that they accomplish assigned missions. It also includes authority to use assigned equipment and resources to accomplish your

FM 7-22.7

missions. Remember that this only applies to soldiers and facilities in your unit. For example, if the platoon sergeant of first platoon goes on leave and a squad leader is put in charge, that squad leader has command authority over only first platoon, until he is relieved from the responsibility. The soldiers in first platoon will obey the squad leader's orders due to his position. However, the squad leader does not have command authority over another platoon.

> *"As a leader... you are not given authority, status and position as a personal reward to enjoy in comfort. You are given them so that you may be of greater service to your subordinates, your unit and your country."*
>
> FM 22-100, *Army Leadership* (1983)

2-24. **General military authority** is authority extended to all soldiers to take action and act in the absence of a unit leader or other designated authority. It originates in oaths of office, law, rank structure, traditions and regulations. This broad-based authority also allows leaders to take appropriate corrective actions whenever a member of any armed service, anywhere, commits an act involving a breach of good order or discipline. For example, if you see soldiers in a brawl, you have the general military authority (and the obligation) to stop the fight. This authority applies even if none of the soldiers are in your unit.

2-25. General military authority exists whether you are on duty or not, in uniform or in civilian attire and regardless of location. For example, you are off duty, in civilian clothes and in the PX and you see a soldier in uniform with his headgear raised up and trousers unbloused. You stop the soldier immediately, identify yourself and ensure the soldier understands and makes the necessary corrections. If he refuses, saying you don't have the authority to tell him what to do because he's not in your NCO support channel, *the soldier is wrong.*.

2-26. You as an NCO have both general military authority and the duty to enforce standards as outlined in AR 670-1. Your authority to enforce those regulations is specified in AR 600-20 and if you neglect your duty, you can be held accountable. If the soldier refuses to obey you, what can you do? For starters, you can explain that you have authority regardless of your location, your unit, or whether you are in uniform or civilian attire. You may decide to settle for the soldier's name and unit. If so, a phone call to his first sergeant should be more than enough to ensure that such an incident does not recur.

> *"Speak with your own voice."*
>
> CSM Clifford R. West

2-27. **Delegation of authority.** Just as Congress and the President cannot participate in every aspect of the armed forces operations, most leaders cannot

Duties, Responsibilities and Authority of the NCO

handle every action directly. To meet the organization's goals, officers delegate authority to NCOs in the NCO Support Channel who, in turn, may further delegate that authority. Unless restricted by law, regulation, or a superior, leaders may delegate any or all of their authority to their subordinate leaders. However, such delegation must fall within the leader's scope of authority. Leaders cannot delegate authority they do not have and subordinate leaders may not assume authority that superiors do not have, cannot delegate, or have retained. The task or duty to be performed limits the authority of the leader to whom it is assigned.

2-28. Both command and general military authority originate in the Constitution and Congress has further defined them in law. More explicit sources are Army Regulations, the Manual for Courts Martial (MCM) and the chain of command/NCO support channel.

2-29. You don't need to read or remember all Army Regulations (ARs) but study those that pertain to your job. If necessary, ask other NCOs to help you find out what regulations pertain to you, where they can be found and how to interpret them. Start with AR 600–20. It covers enlisted soldiers' and noncommissioned officers' authority and responsibilities.

2-30. The Manual for Courts Martial (MCM, 2002) describes legal aspects of the authority of the noncommissioned officer. It states in part that, "All commissioned officers, warrant officers and noncommissioned officers are authorized to stop quarrels, frays and disorders among persons subject to the code...." Severe penalties are imposed for violations such as disrespect, insubordination, or assault. No one expects you to be an expert on military law, but as a noncommissioned officer you should know the definition of these words and be able to explain them to your soldiers. Your legal clerk can be a good source of information.

Authority of the NCO is part of the equation in military discipline.

2-31. Your authority also stems from the combination of the chain of command and the NCO support channel. Orders and policies that pass through the chain of command or the NCO support channel automatically provide the authority necessary to get the job done. With such broad authority given to all commissioned officers and noncommissioned officers, the responsibility to use mature, sound judgment is critical. The chain of command backs up the NCO support channel by legally punishing those who challenge the NCO's authority. But it does so only if the noncommissioned officer's actions and orders are sound, intelligent and based on proper authority. To be a good leader, you should learn what types of authority you have and where it comes from. Whenever in doubt, ask. Once you're confident that you know the extent

FM 7-22.7

of your authority, use sound judgment in applying it. Then you will be a leader respected by both your soldiers and superiors.

INSPECTIONS AND CORRECTIONS

2-32. Why do we have inspections? From long experience, the Army has found that some soldiers, if allowed to, will become careless and lax in the performance of minor barrack duties in their unit. They become accustomed to conditions in their immediate surroundings and overlook minor deficiencies. Should a soldier fall below the Army standard of performance, you can be assured that someone will notice those deficiencies immediately.

2-33. Your superiors will order inspections to see that soldiers have all the equipment and clothing issued to them and that it is serviceable. Inspections serve this practical purpose; they are not harassment. You will probably agree that inspections often correct small problems before they become big problems. Sharp appearance, efficient performance and excellent maintenance are important considerations that affect you directly. They are the earmarks of a good organization and one you should be a proud member of. First line

_____ **Duties, Responsibilities and Authority of the NCO**

leaders should inspect their soldiers daily and should regularly check soldiers' rooms in the barracks. First line leaders should also make arrangements with soldiers who live in quarters (on or off post) to ensure the soldier maintains a healthy and safe environment for himself and his family.

TYPES OF INSPECTIONS

2-34. There are two categories of inspections for determining the status of individual soldiers and their equipment: in-ranks and in-quarters. An in-ranks inspection is of personnel and equipment in a unit formation. The leader examines each soldier individually, noticing their general appearance and the condition of their clothing and equipment. When inspecting crew-served weapons and vehicles, the personnel are normally positioned to the rear of the formation with the operators standing by their vehicle or weapon. Leaders may conduct an in-quarters (barracks) inspection to include personal appearance, individual weapons, field equipment, displays, maintenance and sanitary conditions. Organizations will have inspection programs that help determine the status and mission readiness of the unit and its components. These include Command Inspections, Staff Inspections and Inspector General Inspections.

- The training, instruction, or correction given to a soldier to correct deficiencies must be directly related to the deficiency.
- Orient the corrective action to improving the soldier's performance in their problem area.
- You may take corrective measures after normal duty hours. Such measures assume the nature of the training or instruction, not punishment.
- Corrective training should continue only until the training deficiency is overcome.
- All levels of command should take care to ensure that training and instruction are not used in an oppressive manner to evade the procedural safeguards in imposing nonjudical punishment.
- Do not make notes in soldiers' official records of deficiencies satisfactorily corrected by means of training and instruction.

Figure 2-3. On-the-Spot Correction Guidelines

2-35. **On-the-Spot Corrections.** One of the most effective administrative corrective measures is on-the-spot correction. Use this tool for making the quickest and often most effective corrections to deficiencies in training or standards. Generally there is one of two reasons a soldier requires an on-the-spot correction. Either the soldier you are correcting does not know what the standard is or does not care what the standard is. If the soldier was aware of the standard but chose not to adhere to it, this may indicate a larger problem that his chain of command should address. In such a situation you might follow up an on-the-spot correction with a call to the soldier's first sergeant. Figure 2-3 provides guidelines on making an on-the-spot correction.

> **SGT Park and the On-the-Spot Correction**
>
> As SGT Park left the Dining Facility after breakfast one morning, he stopped to buy a paper from a newspaper machine nearby. Just as he let go of the machine door, letting it slam shut, a soldier (who was about 30 feet away) shouted, "Hey! Hold it Open!" When the soldier saw SGT Park had let it close he said, "Thanks a lot, pal."
>
> SGT Park called the soldier over, identified himself and his unit and asked if the soldier knew the proper way to address an NCO. The soldier said he hadn't realized that SGT Park was an NCO and would have addressed him by his rank if he had. Then SGT Park asked him if he was aware that taking a newspaper without paying for it was theft. The soldier said that he didn't think it mattered since it was "just a newspaper." SGT Park told him that it did matter, just as proper execution of seemingly small, unimportant tasks matters to the Army as a whole. The soldier, who was at parade rest and respectful throughout the conversation, nodded and said, "Alright, sergeant."
>
> SGT Park ended the on-the-spot correction by asking the soldier to think about what integrity meant and whether a soldier's honesty is important to the Army.

2-36. Keeping a soldier on track is the key element in solving performance problems. Motivated soldiers keep the group functioning, training productive and ultimately, accomplish the training objectives and most importantly the mission. Some leaders believe that soldiers work as expected simply because that is their job. That may be true. But soldiers and leaders need a simple pat on back once in a while, for a job well done. You need to praise your soldiers and let them know that you care about the job they are doing and you are glad they are part of the team. Soldiers not performing to standard need correction; use the on-the-spot correction tool. Even after making an on-the-spot correction additional training may be necessary. Figure 2-4 shows the steps in making an on-the-spot correction.

- Correct the soldier.
- Attack the performance, never the person.
- Give one correction at a time. Do not dump.
- Don't keep bringing it up — when the correction is over, it is over.

Figure 2-4. On-the-Spot Correction Steps

2-37. More often than not, your soldiers do good things that deserve a pat on the back. In the same way you do on-the-spot corrections (but obviously for

Duties, Responsibilities and Authority of the NCO

different reasons), praise your soldiers' good work by telling them the specific action or result observed, why it was good and encourage the soldier to continue. Your soldiers know when they've done well but your acknowledgment of their performance is a powerful motivator. It reinforces standards, builds soldiers' pride and lets them know you notice the hard work they do. It is also another indicator that you care about them.

> *"Correct errors in the use of judgment and initiative in such a way as to encourage the individual."*
>
> FM 22-10, *Leadership* (1951)

2-38. **On-the-Spot Inspections.** Making an informal, unscheduled check of equipment, soldiers or quarters is called an on-the-spot inspection. Stopping to check the tag on a fire extinguisher as you walk through a maintenance bay is an example of an on-the-spot inspection. Another example is checking the condition of the trash dumpster area in back of the orderly room. For any inspection, the steps are the same.

- Preparation.
- Conduct.
- Follow-up.

2-39. **PCC/PCI.** Pre-combat checks (PCCs) / Pre-combat inspections (PCIs) and Pre-execution checks are key to ensuring leaders, trainers and soldiers are adequately prepared to execute operations and training to Army standard. PCC/ PCIs are the bridge between pre-execution checks and execution of training. They are also detailed final checks that all units conduct before and during execution of training and combat operations. Conduct PCC/PCIs at the beginning of each event or exercise as part of troop leading procedures to check personnel, equipment, vehicles and mission knowledge. The chain of command is responsible for developing, validating and verifying all PCC/PCIs. Pre-execution checks ensure that all planning and prerequisite training (soldier, leader and collective) are complete prior to the execution of training. They systematically prepare soldiers, trainers and resources to ensure training execution starts properly. Pre-execution checks provide the attention to detail needed to use resources efficiently.

2-40. You are the key to inspections, checking soldier and unit readiness in personal hygiene and appearance, weapons, field equipment, displays and sanitary conditions. Inspections must be done regularly to help reinforce standards and instill discipline. Regular, impartial inspections of important areas develop confidence, teamwork and soldiers' pride in themselves and their equipment.

FM 7-22.7

NONCOMMISSIONED, COMMISSIONED AND WARRANT OFFICER RELATIONSHIPS

2-41. An important part of your role as an NCO is how you relate to commissioned officers. To develop this working relationship, NCOs and officers must know the similarities of their respective duties and responsibilities.

2-42. Commissioned officers hold a commission from the President of the United States, which authorizes them to act as the President's representative in certain military matters. Laws, regulations, policies and customs limit the duties and responsibilities of commissioned officers, like NCOs and other government officials. As the President's representatives, commissioned officers carry out the orders of the Commander in Chief as they are handed down through the chain of command. In carrying out orders, commissioned officers get considerable help, advice and assistance from NCOs. Both commissioned officers and NCOs share the same goal – accomplish the unit's mission. Figure 2-5 lists general duties of commissioned officers.

The Commissioned Officer

- Commands, establishes policy, plans and programs the work of the Army.
- Concentrates on collective training, which will enable the unit to accomplish its mission.
- Is primarily involved with unit operations, training and related activities.
- Concentrates on unit effectiveness and unit readiness.
- Pays particular attention to the standards of performance, training and professional development of officers as well as NCOs.
- Creates conditions – makes the time and other resources available – so the NCO can do the Job.
- Supports the NCO.

Figure 2-5. General Duties of Commissioned Officers

2-43. Warrant officers are highly specialized, single-tracked specialty officers who receive their authority from the Secretary of the Army upon their initial appointment. However, Title 10 USC authorizes the commissioning of Warrant Officers (WO1) upon promotion to Chief Warrant Officer (CW2). These commissioned warrant officers are direct representatives of the President of the United States. They derive their authority from the same source as commissioned officers but remain specialists, in contrast to commissioned officers who are generalists. Figure 2-6 lists general duties of warrant officers.

_____Duties, Responsibilities and Authority of the NCO

The Warrant Officer

- Provides quality advice, counsel and solutions to support the command.
- Executes policy and manages the Army's system.
- Commands special-purpose units and tasks-organized operational elements.
- Focuses on collective, leader and individual training.
- Operates, maintains, administers and manages the Army's equipment, support activities and technical system.
- Concentrates on unit effectiveness and readiness.
- Supports the NCO.

Figure 2-6. General Duties of Warrant Officers

2-44. Warrant officers can and do command detachments, units, activities and vessels as well as lead, coach, train and counsel soldiers. As leaders and technical/tactical experts, warrant officers provide valuable skills, guidance and expertise to commanders and organizations in their particular field.

2-45. Warrant officers provide mentorship, leadership and training to NCOs to support technical, tactical and mission-related tasks. The relationship between the warrant officer and NCO is similar to the commissioned officer. They rely on each other for help, advice and assistance to accomplish the unit's mission.

The Noncommissioned Officer

- Conducts the daily business of the Army within established orders, directives and policies.
- Focuses on individual training, which develops the capability to accomplish the mission.
- Primarily involved with training and leading soldiers and teams.
- Ensures each subordinate team, NCO and soldier are prepared to function as a effective unit and each team member is well trained, highly motivated, ready and functioning.
- Concentrates on standards of performance, training and professional development of NCOs and enlisted soldiers.
- Follows orders of officers and NCOs in the support channel.
- Gets the job done.

Figure 2-7. General Duties of Noncommissioned Officers

2-46. Noncommissioned officers, the backbone of the Army, train, lead and take care of enlisted soldiers. They receive their authority from their oaths of office, law, rank structure, duty position, traditions and regulations. This authority allows them to direct soldiers, take actions required to accomplish the mission and enforce good order and discipline. NCOs represent officer and sometimes DA civilian leaders. They ensure their soldiers, along with their personal equipment, are prepared to function as an effective unit and team members. While commissioned officers command, establish policy and manage resources, NCOs conduct the Army's daily business. Figure 2-7 lists general duties of NCOs.

SPECIAL MENTION

2-47. Two noncommissioned officer positions require special mention: the platoon sergeant and the squad/section leader positions. The platoon sergeant's position is unique because the platoon sergeant must be ready to assume the responsibilities of the platoon leader — an officer. The platoon sergeant takes command in the platoon leader's absence. Therefore, the platoon sergeant's tasks are essentially the same as those of the platoon leader. As acting platoon leader, the platoon sergeant assumes the same responsibilities as the commissioned officer. The platoon leader and platoon sergeant must understand each other; the platoon sergeant must be able to move in and out of the officer's area of responsibility to prepare to replace the platoon leader if necessary. In many cases, the platoon sergeant has much more experience than the lieutenant does; one important task is to teach and advise the lieutenant. The platoon needs both the officer and the sergeant and they must know each other without thinking.

> *There is naturally some overlap of duties and responsibilities between officers and NCOs. This is a necessary and desirable outcome of close cooperation and should be a source of strength for a unit rather than the cause of friction.*

2-48. The second unique position is the squad, section or team leader. Possibly the only NCO in the squad, section or team, he is **the** leader of his soldiers. This NCO is the first link in both the NCO support channel and chain of command. They take their orders from both the platoon sergeant and platoon leader. This is another reason why the platoon sergeant and platoon leader must know what each other are doing. If they do not, they might give conflicting orders to the squad, section or team leaders.

2-49. Noncommissioned, commissioned and warrant officers depend on each other and work together to accomplish the mission of the unit. It is impossible

_____ **Duties, Responsibilities and Authority of the NCO**

for an officer to command an effective unit and accomplish the mission if the NCO doesn't ensure the soldiers know their jobs. Commissioned officers, warrant officers and NCOs must advise, assist and learn from each other. Although the officer is held accountable for all that the unit does or fails to do, only by working together with the NCO can he assure the job will get accomplished.

THE NONCOMMISSIONED OFFICER SUPPORT CHANNEL

2-50. The NCO support channel is subordinate to and supportive of the chain of command. The NCO support channel is not an independent channel. It is incumbent on the users of this channel to ensure that the chain of command is kept informed of actions implemented through the NCO support channel and to eliminate the possibility of the NCO support channel operating outside of command policy and directives. Problems should be brought to the attention of the chain of command and resolved through a coordinated effort. Since the NCO support channel should be operating in accordance with established command policy and directives, conflicts should be minimal and easily resolved.

2-51. Prior to 1977 the NCO support channel was regarded as informal. However, AR 600-20 formalized the NCO support channel and expanded its functions in December 1976. The NCO support channel is now directive in nature within established policies and orders. Because of this, commanders are seeing the senior NCO more actively participating in all unit activities and tasks. The NCO support channel (leadership chain) parallels and reinforces the chain of command. NCO leaders work with and support the commissioned and warrant officers of their chain of command.

2-52. In units at the battalion level and higher, the NCO support channel is the communication and supervision that begins with the command sergeant major (CSM), extends through first sergeants and platoon sergeants and ends with section chiefs, squad leaders, or team leaders. *In addition to passing information, this channel is used for executing the commander's orders and getting routine, but important, jobs done.* Most often it is used to put into effect policies and procedures and to enforce standards of performance, training, appearance and conduct.

2-53. The connection between the chain of command and the NCO support channel is the senior NCO. Commanders issue orders through the chain of command, but senior NCOs must know and understand the orders to issue effective implementing instructions through the NCO support channel. Although the first sergeant and command sergeants major are not part of the

2-17

FM 7-22.7

formal chain of command, leaders should consult them on individual soldier matters.

2-54. Successful officers have a good leader and NCO relationship with their first sergeants and command sergeants major. This leaves the commander free to plan, make decisions and program future training and operations. The need for such a relationship applies to platoon leaders and platoon sergeants as well as to staff officers and NCOs. Senior NCOs have extensive experience in successfully completing missions and dealing with enlisted soldier issues. Also, senior NCOs can monitor organizational activities at all levels, take corrective action to keep the organization within the boundaries of the commander's intent, or report situations that require the attention of the officer leadership. ***Regardless of where the information or task begins – in the chain of command or in the NCO support channel – keep the counterpart informed.*** A positive relationship between officers and NCOs creates conditions for success.

2-55. The NCO support channel assists the chain of command in accomplishing the following:

- Transmitting, instilling and ensuring the efficacy of the professional Army ethic.
- Planning and conducting the day-to-day unit operations within prescribed policies and directives.
- Training enlisted soldiers in their MOS as well as in the basic skills and attributes of a soldier.
- Supervising unit physical fitness training and ensuring that soldiers comply with the weight and appearance standards in AR 600-9 and AR 670-1.
- Teaching soldiers the history of the Army, to include military customs, courtesies and traditions.
- Caring for individual soldiers and their families both on and off duty.
- Teaching soldiers the mission of the unit and developing individual training programs to support the mission.
- Accounting for and maintaining individual arms and equipment of enlisted soldiers and unit equipment under their control.
- Administering and monitoring the NCO professional development program and other unit training programs.
- Achieving and maintaining Army Values.
- Advising the commander on rewards and punishment for enlisted soldiers.

2-56. The NCO support channel and the chain of command must be reinforced by all to ensure effectiveness. It is the channel of communication and supervision from the command sergeant major to the most junior enlisted soldier in the unit. Commanders may further specify responsibilities and

Duties, Responsibilities and Authority of the NCO

authority of their NCOs to their staffs and subordinates. Your contribution to the NCO support channel ensures its overall success.

> *"...the routine daily business of the Army is noncommissioned officer business, that is to say, execution of established policies and standards pertaining to the performance, training and conduct of enlisted personnel is the responsibility of the Noncommissioned Officer Corps. The establishment of those policies and standards is the responsibility of the officer corps."*
>
> CSM J. F. La Voie

NCO RANKS

SERGEANT MAJOR OF THE ARMY

2-57. Established in 1966, the Sergeant Major of the Army (SMA) is the senior enlisted position of the Army. The sergeant major in this position serves as the senior enlisted advisor and consultant to the Chief of Staff of the Army. The SMA provides information on problems affecting enlisted personnel and proposes solutions to these problems concerning standards, professional development, growth and advancement of NCOs, morale, training, pay, promotions and quality of life for soldiers and family members.

2-58. Using command information channels, the SMA keeps soldiers current on important NCO issues and through the public media informs the American people of the Army mission, soldiers' accomplishments and future enlisted trends. The SMA directs NCO support channel activities through the major commands' CSMs by using written and verbal communications. The SMA also presents the enlisted viewpoint to Congress, DA boards and committees, meets with military and civilian organizations to discuss enlisted affairs, and receives and represents Army enlisted personnel at appropriate ceremonies.

COMMAND SERGEANT MAJOR AND SERGEANT MAJOR

2-59. The Command Sergeant Major is the senior NCO of the command at battalion or higher levels. The CSM carries out policies and standards on performance, training, appearance and conduct of enlisted personnel. The CSM gives advice and initiates recommendations to the commander and staff in matters pertaining to enlisted personnel. A unit, installation, or higher headquarters CSM directs the activities of that NCO support channel. The support channel functions orally through the CSMs or first sergeant's call and normally does not involve written instruction. The CSM administers the unit Noncommissioned Officer Development Program (NCODP), normally through written directives and the NCO support channel. As the senior NCO of the command, the CSM is the training professional within the unit, overseeing and driving the entire training program. The CSM assists the commander in determining leader tasks and training for NCOs.

FM 7-22.7 _____

2-60. The CSM and commander jointly coordinate and develop the unit's Mission Essential Task List (METL) and individual training tasks to create a team approach to battle-focused training. The CSM and NCO leaders then select the specific individual tasks, which support each collective task to be trained during this same period. CSMs use command information channels to inform, express concerns on enlisted issues and build esprit. They also represent the commander at military and civilian functions to maintain good community relations.

2-61. The Sergeant Major is often the key enlisted member of the staff elements at battalion and higher levels. The sergeant major's experience and ability are equal to that of the unit command sergeant major, but leadership influence is generally limited to those directly under their charge. The sergeant major is a subject matter expert in his technical field, primary advisor on policy development, analytical reviewer of regulatory guidance and often fulfills the duties of the command sergeant major in his absence. Sergeants major also serve in non-staff and leadership positions such as Special Forces Team Sergeant Major, instructor at the Sergeants Major Academy or as the State Senior Enlisted Advisor.

Colors and Color Guards

Flags are almost as old as civilization itself. Imperial Egypt and the armies of Babylon and Assyria followed the colors of their kings. Ancient texts mention banners and standards. The flag that identified nations usually were based on the personal or family heraldry of the reigning monarch. As autocracies faded or disappeared, dynastic colors were no longer suitable and national flags came into being. These national flags such as the Union Jack of Great Britain, the Tricolor of France and the Stars and Stripes are relatively new to history. When the struggle for independence united the colonies, there grew a desire for a single flag to represent the new Nation. The first flag borne by our Army representing the 13 colonies was the grand union flag. It was raised over the Continental Army at Cambridge, Massachusetts, on 2 January 1776. The Stars and Stripes as we now know it was born on 14 June 1777.

The flags carried by Color-bearing units are called the national and organizational colors. The Colors may be carried in any formation in which two or more company honor guards or representative elements of a command participate. The Command Sergeant Major is responsible for the safeguarding, care and display of the organizational color. He is also responsible for the selection, training and performance of the Color bearers and Color guards.

The honorary position for the CSM is two steps to the rear and centered on the Color guard.

_____ **Duties, Responsibilities and Authority of the NCO**

> Because of the importance and visibility of the task, it is an honor to be a member of the Color guard. The detail may consist of three to eight soldiers, usually NCOs. The senior (Color) sergeant carries the National Color and commands the Color guard unless a person is designated as the Color sergeant. The Color sergeant gives the necessary commands for the movements and for rendering honors. The most important aspect of the selection, training and performance of the Color guard is the training. Training requires precision in drills, manual of arms, customs and courtesies and wear and appearance of uniforms and insignia.
>
> A well trained color guard at the front of unit's formation signifies a sense of teamwork, confidence, pride, alertness, attention to detail, esprit de corps and discipline. The Color Guard detail should perform its functions as much as possible in accordance with ARs 600-25, 670-1 and 840-10 and FM 22-5.

FIRST SERGEANT AND MASTER SERGEANT

2-62. The First Sergeant is the senior NCO in companies, batteries and troops. The position of first sergeant is similar to that of the CSM in importance, responsibility and prestige. As far back as the Revolutionary War period, first sergeants have enforced discipline, fostered loyalty and commitment in their soldiers, maintained duty rosters and made morning reports to their company commanders. Since today's first sergeants maintain daily contact with and are responsible for training and ensuring the health and welfare of all of the unit's soldiers and families, this position requires extraordinary leadership and professional competence.

2-63. First sergeants hold formations, instruct platoon sergeants and assist the commander in daily unit operations. Though first sergeants supervise routine administrative duties their principle duty is training soldiers. The CSM, first sergeant and other key NCOs, must understand the organization's collective mission essential tasks during METL-based training. Through NCO development programs, performance counseling and other guidance, first sergeants are the Army's most important mentors in developing subordinate NCOs.

2-64. The Master Sergeant serves as the principle NCO in staff elements at battalion or higher levels. Although not charged with the enormous leadership responsibilities of the first sergeant, the master sergeant dispatches leadership and executes other duties with the same professionalism as the first sergeant.

PLATOON SERGEANT AND SERGEANT FIRST CLASS

2-65. While "Platoon Sergeant" is a duty position, not a rank, the platoon sergeant is the primary assistant and advisor to the platoon leader, with the responsibility of training and caring for soldiers. The platoon sergeant helps the commander to train the platoon leader and in that regard has an enormous effect on how that young officer perceives NCOs for the rest of his career. The platoon sergeant takes charge of the platoon in the absence of the platoon leader. As the lowest level senior NCO involved in the company METL, platoon sergeants teach collective and individual tasks to soldiers in their squads, crews or equivalent small units.

2-66. The Sergeant First Class (SFC), may serve in a position subordinate to the platoon sergeant or may serve as the NCO in charge (NCOIC) of the section with all the attendant responsibilities and duties of the platoon sergeant. A platoon sergeant or sergeant first class generally has extensive military experience and can make accurate decisions in the best interest of the mission and the soldier.

2-67. Utilizing tough, realistic and intellectually and physically challenging performance-oriented training to excite and motivate soldiers, the platoon sergeant ensures Army standards are met and maintained. Additionally, the platoon sergeant must conduct cross training to promote critical wartime skills within the unit, evaluate the effectiveness of the platoon and provide training feedback to the commander and first sergeant during After-Action Reviews (AAR) on all unit collective training.

SQUAD, SECTION AND TEAM LEADERS

2-68. Staff Sergeants, Sergeants and Corporals are normally squad, section and team leaders and are a critical link in the NCO channel. These NCOs live and work with their soldiers every day and are responsible for their health, welfare and safety. These squad, section and team leaders ensure that their soldiers meet standards in personal appearance and teach them to maintain and account for their individual and unit equipment and property. The NCO enforces standards and develops and trains soldiers daily in MOS skills and unit missions.

> *"NCOs should make it a point to drop by the barracks on and off duty to visit soldiers and check on their welfare."*

> SMA Jack L. Tilley

2-69. The NCO teaches individual and collective training, develops unit cohesion, fosters the values of loyalty and commitment and builds spirit and confidence. The NCO evaluates performance oriented training and through coaching and counseling grooms young soldiers for future positions of increased responsibility. Squad, section and team leaders teach everything from the making of sound and timely decisions to physical training to ethics and values. You, corporals and sergeants, are the basic trainer of today's soldiers.

_____Duties, Responsibilities and Authority of the NCO

YOU ARE A NONCOMMISSIONED OFFICER

2-70. You as an NCO have a tough, demanding, but very rewarding job. The soldiers you lead are the heart of the Army. You lead soldiers at the action level where the important day-to-day fundamental work of the Army is mission oriented. Because you live and work directly with and among soldiers, you have the best opportunity to know them as they really are. You are the first to identify and teach soldiers how to best use their strengths and help them detect and overcome their shortcomings. You are in the best position to secure the trust and confidence of soldiers by leading by example. You have the advantage of a deeper understanding of soldier behavior because you were promoted directly from the ranks that you now lead and serve. Your soldiers will challenge you each and every day and you will be rewarded by the respect they hold for your ability as a leader. You will be successful as they follow your leadership in the difficult business of getting ready to fight and win our Nation's wars.

approach problems you face. Knowledge of military history is a good confidence builder.

> *"A man cannot lead without determination, without the will and the desire to lead. He cannot do it without studying, reading, observing, learning. He must apply himself to gain the goal- to develop the talent for military leadership.... Leaders are developed! They are guided by others; but they are made-largely self-made."*
>
> MSG Frank K. Nicolas

3-5. Observe other leaders in your unit, especially those who are successful. Learn from them by observing and asking questions. Study yourself too, learning from your own successes and failures. Everyone who wears the uniform of the US Army must be a WARRIOR, first and last. In today's operational environment, there are no front lines; there is no secure rear area. Every soldier must be prepared to attack or defend and win regardless of the conditions. That means conducting full spectrum operations including offense, defense, stability and support. Our Nation depends on the NCO to prepare soldiers to do so.

BE – KNOW – DO

3-6. Noncommissioned officers lead by example. You must BE, KNOW and DO to be effective. However, there are some basics involved here: Character — Competence — Actions.

BE

3-7. Character is an inner strength that helps you know what is right and what is wrong. It is what gives you the desire and fortitude to do what is right even in the toughest situations and it gives you the courage to keep doing what is right regardless of the consequences.

> *"The test of character is not 'hanging in' when you expect light at the end of the tunnel, but performance of duty and persistence of example when you know no light is coming."*
>
> ADM James B. Stockdale

3-8. Others see character in you by your behavior. What you do speaks louder than what you say — set the example. Understand Army values and live them. Develop leader attributes and teach these to your soldiers. This may or may not be easy, but it is vitally important to the success of the Army, your unit and your soldiers.

_____ **Leadership**

"The Army [depends] on competent people who have the strength of character to secure our vital national interests and the foresight to continue change to remain the world's best."

GEN John N. Abrams

3-9. One of the most obvious ways to demonstrate character is to be honest. Tell it like it is – not how you think someone wants to hear it. The Army and your soldiers want, need and deserve the truth. If you make a mistake, admit it; don't sacrifice your integrity. If something is wrong, you must be willing to say so, even to superior NCOs and officers. Do so in an objective, straightforward manner; present the facts. This often takes moral courage. What you have to say may not be easy or even welcomed, but your candor is necessary to develop and maintain trust. It is also necessary for soldiers to know whether they have met the standard and for leaders to know the true status of units. A mark of loyalty is a burning desire to help the unit and one's soldiers get better at their tasks. That demands honesty. Make it a habit to be candid – in battle, lives will depend on it.

"It has long seemed to me that the hard decisions are not the ones you make in the heat of battle. Far harder to make are those involved in speaking your mind about some hare-brained scheme which proposes to commit troops to action under conditions where failure seems almost certain and the only results will be the needless sacrifice of priceless lives."

GEN Matthew B. Ridgway

KNOW

3-10. You need to know a great deal to properly lead soldiers. You must have a number of skills to train soldiers and to lead them in tough situations. Know how to talk to your soldiers and get them to talk. Be able to think and plan ahead and be able to visualize events before they occur. Know everything about your equipment and tactics and how to make decisions based on the information you have available.

Know Your Job

3-11. To be a good noncommissioned officer you must know your job exceptionally well. This means you must be proficient in the employment, care, cleaning and maintenance of vehicles, weapons and equipment assigned to your unit — technical skills. As Army Transformation progresses, you may receive new equipment, learn new doctrine, or undergo organizational changes. You will certainly have to absorb and pass on larger and larger quantities of information. Know all the tactics your unit uses in battle. Realize that in the contemporary operational environment, there are no secure areas – an enemy might attack a logistics site in the rear areas as readily as a frontline leaders become casualties. Make sure your soldiers are ready if you die in battle – one of them has to lead the others or they could all be casualties and the unit will fail in its mission.

Build the team

3-30. The Army is a team. Each of its organizations and units are themselves teams making up the Army. You build teamwork and unit proficiency to prepare for the day when your unit will have to fight. It's important to realize that the national cause, the purpose of the mission and other larger issues probably won't be evident from the battlefield. It's therefore equally important to know that soldiers will perform their duties for the other people in their squad, section or team. Your job as an NCO is to bring each member into the team because you may someday ask that person for extraordinary effort.

3-31. Teambuilding starts with your competence as a leader. Training together builds collective competence and trust is a product of that competence. Soldiers learn to trust their leaders if the leaders know how to do their jobs and act consistently — if they say what they mean and mean what they say — and that trust builds confidence. Continued training to standard makes your soldiers confident in themselves and – this is key – confident in each other because they know they can depend on each other.

> *"You must give [soldiers] reasons to have confidence and pride in themselves, in their leaders and in their units. Only then will you have loyalty."*
>
> SMA George W. Dunaway

3-32. Leaders and soldiers all have contributions in teambuilding. Figure 3-2 lists actions you must do to pull a team together, get it going in the right direction and keep it moving. And that list only hints at the work that lies ahead as you get your team to work together. Teambuilding also occurs in athletics, social activities and unit functions like a Dining-In or Dining-Out. Ultimately, each of your soldiers must know that their contribution is important and valued. They must know that you'll train them and listen to their concerns. They don't want you to let them get away with substandard performance. So constantly observe, counsel, develop and listen; you must be every bit the team player you want your soldiers to be — and more.

_____ Leadership

TEAM BUILDING STAGES

	SUBORDINATE CHALLENGES	LEADER & ORGANIZATION ACTIONS
FORMATION STAGE — GENERIC	• Achieve belonging and acceptance • Set personal and family concerns • Learn about leaders and other members	• Listen to and care for subordinates • Design effective reception and orientation • Communicate • Reward positive contributions • Set example
SOLDIER CRITICAL	• Face the uncertainty of war • Cope with fear of unknown injury and death • Adjust to sights and sounds of war • Adjust to separation from home and family	• Talk with each soldier • Reassure with calm presence • Communicate vital safety tips • Provide stable situation • Establish buddy system • Assist soldiers to deal with immediate problems
ENRICHMENT STAGE — GENERIC	• Trust leaders and other members • Find close friends • Learn who is in charge • Accept the way things are done • Adjust to feelings about how things ought to be done • Overcome family-versus-unit conflict	• Trust and encourage trust • Allow growth while keeping control • Identify and channel emerging leaders • Establish clear lines of authority • Establish individual and unit goals • Train as a unit for mission • Build pride through accomplishment • Acquire self-evaluation/self-assessment habits • Be fair and give responsibility
SOLDIER CRITICAL	• Survive • Demonstrate competence • Become a team member quickly • Learn about the enemy • Learn about the battlefield • Avoid life-threatening mistakes	• Train as a unit for combat • Demonstrate competence • Know the soldiers • Pace subordinate battlefield integration • Provide stable unit climate • Emphasize safety awareness for improved readiness
SUSTAINMENT STAGE — GENERIC	• Trust others • Share ideas and feelings freely • Assist other team members • Sustain trust and confidence • Share mission and values	• Demonstrate trust • Focus on teamwork, training & maintaining • Respond to subordinate problems • Devise more challenging training • Build pride and spirit through unit sports, social & spiritual activities
SOLDIER CRITICAL	• Adjust to continuous operations • Cope with casualties • Adjust to enemy actions • Overcome boredom • Avoid rumors • Control fear, anger, despair and panic	• Observe and enforce sleep discipline • Sustain safety awareness • Inform soldiers • Know and deal with soldiers' perceptions • Keep soldiers productively busy • Use in-process reviews (PRs) and After-Action Reviews (AARs) • Act decisively in face of panic

Figure 3-2. The Teambuilding Stages

impact far beyond your actual area of operations. Remember this – success or failure of an operation could be determined by one sentry, patrol leader, truck driver, or gunner. And that soldier could be one of yours.

> *"Discipline is based on pride in the profession of arms, on meticulous attention to details and on mutual respect and confidence. Discipline must be a habit so ingrained that it is stronger than the excitement of battle or the fear of death."*
>
> GEN George S. Patton, Jr.

3-38. Discipline results in accomplishing all tasks well, even the routine, simple ones.

The Deployment

An infantry battalion had convoyed to an assembly area in preparation to be airlifted. The Air Force crew had difficulty getting the S-1 section's vehicles — two HMMWVs with a water buffalo between them — loaded and properly secured on the C-130. When the crews finished loading and securing the vehicles and cargo, they let the passengers board.

"There were 10 of us and there wasn't much room," says the NCOIC. "I warned my guys, 'don't sit around these vehicles; I don't trust them.' I had a clerk move from between the water buffalo and the rear HMMWV. As the aircraft started to taxi, I woke another soldier who was lying in the rear of the forward HMMWV with his legs hanging out the rear of the truck and had him move his legs inside the vehicle."

Just as the C-130 lifted off the ground, the water buffalo broke loose, rolled back and slammed into the rear HMMWV, breaking its chains and causing both to slam into the rear ramp of the aircraft. The aircrew quickly alerted the flight crew. The pilot immediately set the aircraft back down and braked hard. Both loose vehicles rolled forward, slamming into the truck in the front of the cargo bay.

"There was no serious damage to the vehicles," said the NCOIC, "but I was glad that our soldiers had not been between the trucks or trailers."

INTENDED AND UNINTENDED CONSEQUENCES

3-39. The actions you take as a leader will most likely have unintended as well as intended consequences. Think through what you expect to happen as a result of a decision. Some decisions set off a chain of events; as far as possible, anticipate the effects of your decisions. Even small unit leaders' actions may have effects well beyond what they expect.

3-40. Intended consequences are those results of a leader's decisions and actions the leader anticipated. For example, a convoy has come to a bridge and

_____ Leadership

the convoy commander, concerned about the weight capacity of the bridge, orders his convoy across one vehicle at a time. The intended consequence is for all vehicles to cross safely without damage to the bridge.

3-41. Unintended consequences are unanticipated results of a leader's decisions and actions. For example, if a convoy is lined up in front of the bridge waiting for each vehicle to cross, an intended consequence (because you could foresee it) is that the civilian traffic on the road gets backed up. An unintended (and unforeseen) consequence is that some civilian drivers begin passing the convoy in an unsafe manner.

3-42. All leaders' decisions and actions result in consequences, both intended and unintended. So as a leader you must think through decisions and then do your duty. Try to foresee as far as possible what will result from actions and decisions you take. The leader of a small unit can and often does have an effect on much bigger events.

> *"In today's operational environment, tactical actions by lieutenants, sergeants, corporals and their commanders can have strategic consequences with lasting impact on national policy."*
>
> LTG William M. Steele

PUTTING IT TOGETHER

3-43. The Army leadership framework (Figure 3-1, page 72) is the Army's common basis for thinking about leadership. There is a lot to think about, but the framework gives you the big picture and helps put your job, your people and your organization in perspective. The values, attributes, skills and actions that support **BE**, **KNOW** and **DO** each contain components and all are

3-17

interrelated; none stands alone. For more information on how it fits together and the pieces that comprise the Framework see FM 6-22 (22-100), chapters 1-5. Its pieces work in combination to produce something more than the sum of the parts. **BE** the leader of character: live Army values and demonstrate leader attributes. Study and practice so that you have the skills to **KNOW** your job. Then act, **DO** what's right to train and care for your soldiers while accomplishing the mission.

> *"One of the things that makes our Army great is that we train and plan for all of our soldiers to be leaders. When the time comes, whether at peace or at war, the American soldier has and will rise to the occasion. Over the years we have seen many changes in our Army — vehicles, weapon systems, uniforms and organizations. However, one thing has not changed- the responsibility entrusted to US Army noncommissioned officers to lead, train, take care of and serve as role models for our soldiers. The greatest privilege is the honor of leading America's finest men and women both in war and peace."*
>
> SMA Julius W. Gates

3-44. Leadership in combat is your primary and most important challenge. It requires you to develop in yourself and your soldiers the ability and the will to win — mental toughness. Check your soldiers' mental toughness. An example of a gut check of mental toughness is taking the formation past the barracks at the end of a four mile run. Army values contribute to a core of motivation and will. Without such motivation and will, your soldiers may die unnecessarily. You are leading a part of the force that will fight and win the Nation's wars and serves the common defense of the United States. In the years ahead, you will be called upon for a variety of missions under extreme conditions. In some cases you'll be doing things you've never done before. But you can and will succeed.

YOU ARE AN NCO!

As a noncommissioned officer, you have been chosen to be a leader; be a good one. Good leadership throughout the Army is the glue that holds units together. Training, practice and experience build good leaders. Be proud you are a leader; strive to be one of the best!

Chapter 4

Training

Noncommissioned officers train soldiers to perform individual soldier tasks to established standards. NCOs also train the small units of the Army – squads, sections, crews, fire teams – to fight together as teams using their equipment effectively.

Training sharpens the mind, builds the spirit and strengthens the team

	Page
NCOs Lay the Foundation in Training	4-3
Battle Focus	4-3
Mission Essential Task List	4-4
Selection of Platoon and Squad Collective Tasks	4-5
Selection of Leader and Soldier Tasks	4-5
Leader's Role in Training	4-6
Planning	4-7
Preparation	4-9
Execution	4-10
Standards	4-12
Other Leader Concerns in Training	4-12
Realism	4-12
Safety	4-13

FM 7-22.7

    Sergeant's Time Training 4-13
    Opportunity Training 4-14
    Drills 4-14
Assessment 4-16
    Assessment Tools 4-16
    Training Meetings 4-17

For more information on training and the NCO's role in it see FM 7-0 (25-100), *Training the Force* **and FM 7-1 (25-101),** *Battle Focused Training.*

NCOS LAY THE FOUNDATION IN TRAINING

4-1. Army training tradition and common sense have made the noncommissioned officer responsible for individual, crew and team training. The first line supervisor teaches individual tasks to soldiers in their squads, crews, or equivalent small units. The first line supervisor and his senior NCOs emphasize performance-oriented practice to ensure soldiers achieve soldier's manual standards. The first line supervisor conducts cross training to spread critical wartime skills within his unit. The CSMs, first sergeants and other senior NCOs coach junior NCOs to master a wide range of individual tasks.

> *"The first line supervisor builds the team at the operational level. The success/failure of the team depends on how well trained this team is, how it performs as a team and what it learns from training as a team. The Junior NCO leads this effort and provides the leadership for building and strengthening the team."*
>
> CSM A. Frank Lever, III

4-2. A good leader develops a genuine concern for the well-being of their soldiers. In the Army, this simply means that leaders must know and understand their soldiers well enough to train them to a high level of proficiency as individuals and team and to have confidence in their ability to perform well under the difficult and demanding conditions of battle. The best way to take care of your soldiers is to train them well. Training is the NCO's principle duty and responsibility: no one has more to do with training soldiers than the noncommissioned officer. The Army can provide ranges, ammunition, soldier's manuals, training aids and devices, but none of these can do the training - they are tools for NCOs to train their soldiers. Good training bonds tactics, weapons, equipment and units to accomplish the mission.

4-3. Commanders allot training time for NCOs to conduct individual training and require that individual tasks are included in all collective Mission Essential Task List (METL) training. Commanders also allot sufficient time so NCOs can retrain soldiers who need it to meet the standard. NCOs are responsible for conducting individual training to standard and must be able to explain how individual task training relates to collective mission essential tasks. NCO leader training occurs in NCO Development Programs (NCODP), collective training, developmental counseling and self-development.

BATTLE FOCUS

4-4. Battle focus is a concept used to determine training requirements from wartime missions. Units cannot achieve and sustain proficiency on all possible soldier, leader and collective tasks. Commanders with NCO assistance selectively identify and train those tasks that accomplish the unit's critical wartime mission. The METL is the focal point for planning, execution and assessment of training. This is critical throughout the entire training process and aids in allocating resources for training. It also enables tailoring of unit leader development training for those competencies required to execute Army warfighting doctrine.

> *"When you're in the Army, you can be in the infantry at any given moment."*
>
> SGT Michael Davis

4-5. NCOs link the collective mission essential tasks and the leader and soldier tasks that support them. The CSM and NCO leaders select specific soldier tasks that support each collective task of the METL. NCOs are primarily responsible for training soldier tasks. Leaders at every level remain responsible for training to established standards during soldier, leader and unit training.

MISSION ESSENTIAL TASK LIST

4-6. After the commander designates the collective mission essential tasks required to accomplish the unit's wartime mission, the CSM and senior NCOs develop a supporting individual task list for each mission essential task. Often called the "METL Crosswalk," soldier training publications and mission training plans are major source documents for selecting appropriate individual tasks.

INTEGRATION OF SOLDIER, LEADER AND COLLECTIVE TRAINING

4-7. The Company/Battery/Troop is the lowest level to have a METL. The commander gives to his chain of command the mission and METL for accomplishing the company's wartime mission.

SELECTION OF PLATOON AND SQUAD COLLECTIVE TASKS

4-8. From the company mission and METL, the platoon leader and platoon sergeant determine their collective tasks. They –

- Use the mission-to-collective task matrix found in the appropriate platoon Army Training Evaluation Program Mission Training Plan (ARTEP MTP) to determine platoon collective tasks that support each company mission essential task.
- Determine which collective tasks support more than one company mission essential task to identify high payoff tasks. For example, most infantry company mission essential tasks require the infantry platoon collective task, "Move Tactically."
- Present selected platoon collective tasks to the company commander to obtain guidance and approval. The commander uses METT-T analysis, resource availability and unit status analysis to select the most important platoon tasks.

4-9. The platoon leader and platoon sergeant assist the squad leaders in determining the squad collective tasks to accomplish the platoon collective tasks. They used the same process as above to select these tasks. The company commander approves the squad collective tasks.

SELECTION OF LEADER AND SOLDIER TASKS

4-10. Unit leaders select soldier tasks to support squad and platoon collective tasks using the collective-to-soldier task matrix found in the appropriate ARTEP MTPs. They do this for each skill level in the unit.

4-11. The CSM and key NCOs review and refine the supporting soldier tasks for each skill level in every MOS within the unit, especially low-density MOS tasks. Leader books are a valuable tool to track task proficiency. Information on the leader book is in Appendix C.

4-12. You can find leader tasks in the appropriate Soldier Training Publication (STP), MTP, or soldier's manual. Company commanders use the appropriate platoon ARTEP MTP to identify platoon leader tasks. The 1SG and key NCOs use appropriate STPs to identify NCO leader tasks. Leaders must be proficient on these and other specified leader tasks before conducting collective training. See Figure 4-1.

FM 7-22.7

Soldier to Be Trained	Task Selection	Review	Approve
1SG	CSM	Co. Cdr	Bn Cdr
PSG	1SG	Plt Ldr/Co. Cdr	Bn Cdr
Sqd Ldr	PSG	Plt Ldr/1SG	Co. Cdr
Tm Ldr	Sqd Ldr	PSG/Plt Ldr	Co. Cdr
Soldier	Tm Ldr	Sqd Ldr/PSG	Plt Ldr

Figure 4-1. Task Approval Matrix

4-13. Combat Support and Combat Service Support leaders have similar documents available. When no published leader tasks exist, develop them using doctrinal manuals, other proponent school publications and common task manuals. The skill level 3 tasks in the food service STP provide CSS leader tasks for a food service NCO, for example –

- Establish layout of field feeding areas.
- Supervise operation and maintenance of the Mobile Kitchen Trailer (MKT).
- Supervise personnel in cleaning and maintenance of field feeding equipment.
- Request and turn-in subsistence.

4-14. All leaders and soldiers must perform common tasks and *essential* Military Occupational Specialty (MOS) - specific tasks. There are 85 common tasks and 70 MOS-specific tasks in ARTEP 7-8-MTP, *Mission Training Plan for the Infantry Rifle Platoon and Squad*. This list of 155 tasks would be too large to sustain because of limited training time and other resource constraints. Leaders use battle focus to refine the list to mission related tasks that are essential to the soldier's duty position and analyze it to eliminate duplication.

> **Corporal Sandy Jones in World War I**
>
> "Corporal Sandy E. Jones [a soldier in one of the black units in WWI], after all his officers had been knocked out and most of his sergeants, put a company together and led it for two days against a hill position. Corporal Jones was the Iron Commander's [GEN John J. Pershing] idea of a fighter...a fighter...a fighter. Pershing pinned the Distinguished Service Cross on his left breast."

LEADER'S ROLE IN TRAINING

4-15. In addition to the commander's responsibilities, all leaders must require their soldiers to understand and perform their roles in training. The commander assigns primary responsibility to officers for collective training and to noncommissioned officers for soldier training. NCOs also have

_____**Training**

responsibility to train squads, sections, teams and crews. The commander melds leader and soldier training requirements into collective training events so that all gain training value from each event. Additionally, all leaders —

- Exchange information. Guidance on missions and priorities flows down; soldier, leader and collective training needs flow up. Training meetings, briefings and AARs are the primary forums for exchanging training information.
- Demand soldiers achieve training standards.
  - Set aside time to training tasks not performed to standard.
  - Plan to train a realistic number of tasks during a training event. It is better to train to standard on a few tasks than fail to achieve the standard on many. *Soldiers will remember the <u>enforced</u> standard.*
- Assess the results of training in the AAR. The leader at every level analyzes the unit and soldiers' performance and makes judgment on their strengths and weaknesses. This may lead to additional training or recommendations for future training events.

4-16. About half of the Army force structure is in the Reserve Component (RC) — the Army National Guard (ARNG) and US Army Reserve (USAR). *RC units train to the same standard on each task as Active units.* However, they train fewer tasks because of reduced training time, geographical dispersion, availability of equipment for training and fewer training areas. Nonetheless, RC units have only two days each month (unit training assemblies) and two weeks of Annual Training (AT) each year in which to conduct training. This requires efficient use of time and resources. NCOs in the RC are among the most dedicated and innovative leaders in the Army and make maximum use of limited resources.

> *"A lot of time, support personnel say, 'we do our wartime mission every day.' That's not so. You've got to look at the conditions in which you're performing those missions."*
>
> CSM Bobby Butler

PLANNING

4-17. Short-range planning is based on the long-range unit assessment and on a detailed training assessment of the unit's current METL proficiency. It focuses on training deficiencies that impact on the unit's ability to perform its wartime mission. A training assessment is—

- Required for each METL task, platoon and squad collective task, soldier task and, at battalion and higher headquarters, each battle task.
- A snapshot of the unit's current soldier, leader and collective task proficiency.
- A comparison of task proficiency with *Army* standards.

FM 7-22.7

4-18. Training meetings are *non-negotiable* at battalion and company level. Battalions and companies must hold them. Training meetings provide guidance for forming training schedules. In the Active Component (AC) the primary focus of training meetings at battalion level is training management issues for the next six weeks while RC units are looking one or two years ahead. Coordination meetings should be held to resolve resource issues prior to the battalion training meeting. At company level, training meetings focus on the specifics of training to be conducted.

4-19. Meetings are also held at platoon and squad level. Essential soldier, leader and collective training needs must be identified and sent up the chain of command. Likewise, information passed out at the company training meeting must reach every soldier through the platoon chain of command. The training schedule provides this detailed information. Training schedules provide predictability for soldiers and create confidence in the chain of command. Near-term planning conducted at the training meeting results in detailed training schedules. The training schedule is the unit's primary management tool to ensure training is conducted on time and by qualified trainers with the necessary resources.

The Training Schedule
Once the battalion commander approves and the company commander signs the training schedule, it is locked in and constitutes an official order

4-20. Only the approving authority can change the training schedule; for example, for the company, it is normally the battalion commander. Higher headquarters must then protect units from unprogrammed events, activities and other distracters. Leaders must ensure daily training is conducted to standard and adheres to the training schedule. CSMs and 1SGs are key to making this happen. Soldiers have a legal responsibility to attend scheduled training.

4-21. Training cannot happen if essential equipment and systems (such as tracks, weapons, wheeled vehicles, or radios) are Nonmission Capable (NMC). Everyone (leaders, maintenance personnel and operators) must be trained and involved to improve and sustain the unit's maintenance posture. In war, soldiers and crews perform Preventive Maintenance Checks and Services (PMCS) under combat conditions often without the normal direction and supervision of superiors. This requires maintenance personnel and equipment or vehicle operators who are proficient in their maintenance duties. Leaders train soldiers to meet Army maintenance standards. NCOs instill an understanding of and the know-how to perform day-to-day maintenance operations.

PREPARATION

4-22. Formal planning for training culminates with the publication of the training schedule. Informal planning, detailed coordination and pre-execution checks continue until the training is performed. Well prepared trainers, soldiers and support personnel are ready to participate and their facilities, equipment and materials are ready to use.

4-23. Proper preparation gives trainers confidence in their ability to train. They must rehearse their preparations and review the tasks and subtasks to be covered during their training. To prepare trainers to conduct performance-oriented training, commanders and leaders provide preparation time so that the trainer can—

- Review references, such as ARTEP 71-2-MTP, soldier's manuals, FMs and TMs to understand tasks, conditions and standards.
- Prepare a Task & Evaluation Outline.
- Gather and prepare training support items, equipment and supplies such as Multiple Integrated Laser Engagement System (MILES), other Training Aids, Devices, Simulator and Simulations (TADSS) and Class III and IX.
- Conduct a reconnaissance of training site.
- Prepare the soldiers for training.

4-24. Commanders and leaders also conduct rehearsals to—

- Identify weak points in the training plan.
- Teach effective training techniques and coach as needed.
- Ensure all safety and environmental considerations are met.
- Determine how the trainer will evaluate the soldiers' or unit's performance at the end of training for compliance with the training objective.
- Assess subordinate trainer competencies and provide developmental feedback to them throughout the training preparation and execution process.
- Give them confidence in their ability to train.

"Good work requires much thought and concentrated thinking is the secret of genius."

SSG Ray H. Duncan

4-25. Leaders use MTPs, soldier's manuals, drill books and similar publications to develop the Training and Evaluation Outline (T&EO). Whenever possible, they use the published T&EO.

4-26. To conduct effective, meaningful training for soldiers, leaders and units, thorough preparation is essential. Leaders themselves must be able to perform the task before trying to teach others. Proper preparation gives them

FM 7-22.7

confidence in their ability to train. After proper planning and preparation are complete, soldiers, leaders and units are ready to execute training to standard.

> ### The 555th Parachute Infantry – 'Triple Nickles'
>
> The Triple Nickles (a misspelling at the time that just stuck) – the 555th Parachute Infantry Battalion — was formed in November 1944. Almost all of the officers, NCOs and enlisted men served in the same unit for years and through hard training they developed camaraderie and respect for each other. Everyone was trained thoroughly from the basics of a soldier's individual survival needs to team tactics for combat. The battalion conducted simulated combat jumps and tactical exercises and in each rotated leader roles to develop leadership skills at the lowest level. During these exercises each soldier had the opportunity to lead and command. In early 1945 the 555th engaged in advanced unit combat training and grew to over four hundred men.
>
> Some of the new arrivals were combat veterans from units in Europe and the Pacific. These veterans, on their way to the unit, had already received not only jump training, but also special advanced training at Fort Benning as riggers, demolition men, jumpmasters or pathfinders. After an intensive two-month training program, the Triple Nickles were ready to take on anybody. But by April 1945 the German armies had collapsed and Americans and Russians met on the Elbe River.
>
> The close of the war in Europe in May 1945 brought the Triple Nickles a change of mission. To combat fires in the western US, some of which were started by enemy 'balloon bombs,' they received new parachute training that included three jumps; two in clearings, one in heavy forest. In mid July, the battalion had qualified as Smoke Jumpers — the Army's only airborne firefighters. Soon their operations would range over seven western states. All missions were risky and tough. Jumping into trees was dangerous and the DZ's were often rough. At night they maintained fire and snake and wild animal watches. The 555th participated in thirty-six fire missions — individual jumps totaled over twelve hundred. By August 1945 the war with Japan was over, the 555th returned to Fort Bragg and became an integral part of the 82nd Airborne.

4-27. Most units in the Army train for combat and develop great skill in their given roles. But when conditions and the needs of the Nation change, units adapt and prepare for new roles – and succeed because of hard training and discipline.

EXECUTION

4-28. Training is the peacetime mission of the Army. The execution of training to standard is the payoff for all other phases of training management. Leader supervision and participation at all levels are essential to the successful execution of training. Battle focused leaders ensure that planned training is started on time and executed vigorously to standard. Leaders assess soldier, leader and unit performance throughout the execution phase. They provide feedback to allow soldiers to learn from their strengths and weaknesses and to subsequently adjust their own training programs.

> *"Survival in combat is not solely a matter of luck. Doing things the right way is more important than luck in coming through a battle alive. And training teaches you to do things the right way.... It's training that defeats the enemy and saves lives."*
>
> SMA William O. Wooldridge

NCOs Make it Happen

4-29. Senior NCOs are responsible for getting soldiers, subordinate leaders and units to the training sites. They ensure that soldiers are at the right location, in the right uniform, with the right equipment, at the right time. Further, senior NCOs ensure—

- Detailed inspections and checks are performed prior to all training.
- Prerequisite training is completed so that soldiers' time is not wasted.
- Leaders are trained and prepared to train their squads, sections, teams, or crews. They *train the trainers*.
- Preliminary training for squad, section, team and crew has the right focus and is executed to Army standard.
- Training includes a realistic number of tasks.
- Soldiers train to standard and meet the training objectives. Special emphasis is on low-density MOSs.
- The schedule allows adequate time to repeat tasks not performed to standard the first time.
- Soldiers are properly motivated and well led.
- Soldiers are present and accounted for, especially during STT.

4-30. NCOs are the primary trainers. They are responsible to—

- Account for their soldiers.
- Know their units' and soldiers' training needs and plan appropriate time to train tasks to standard.
- Conduct a rehearsal.
- Identify and conduct appropriate prerequisite training.
- Ensure training is conducted to standard.
- Retrain soldiers when standards are not met.
- Be properly prepared to conduct opportunity training whenever time is available.

> *"Only perfect practice makes perfect."*
>
> SFC Lydia Mead

FM 7-22.7 _____

4-31. Presentation of training provides soldiers with the specific training objectives (tasks, conditions and standards) to be trained and the evaluation methods to be used. The exact type and amount of information presented prior to performing the task depends on the task and the state of training of the soldiers being trained.

> *"[When an instructor] knows his topic thoroughly, he is eager to pour it out."*
>
> MSG Jose R. Carmona

STANDARDS

4-32. Leaders emphasize accomplishing training to standard by identifying the Army standard and, more importantly, by *demanding that soldiers meet those standards*. They ensure soldiers understand when they have not performed training to standard. Leaders must allow sufficient time to retrain the task until it can be performed correctly.

> *"An NCO must know what right looks like and must prepare. As NCOs we never stop learning and must seek guidance from manuals and our leaders to ensure we know the standard. NCOs must be at the training from preparation to execution through retraining."*
>
> CSM Mary E. Sutherland

OTHER LEADER CONCERNS IN TRAINING

REALISM

4-33. Units should train in peacetime as they will fight during war. Peacetime training must replicate battlefield conditions as closely as resources permit. All training is based on this principle. Leaders must ensure that soldiers are trained to cope with complex, stressful and lethal situations they will encounter in combat. Achieve this by—

- Enforcing high standards.
- Training soldiers, leaders and units in a near wartime environment, not in the classroom.
- Ensuring all training is tactically oriented.
- Ensuring Opposing Forces (OPFOR) use appropriate threat or capabilities based doctrine, tactics and equipment.
- Integrating realistic conditions by increasing the difficulty of tasks, such as—
    - Simulate the loss of key leaders.
    - Use of smoke on the battlefield.
    - Require casualty evacuation.
    - Simulate nuclear, biological, chemical (NBC) situations.
    - Replicate battlefield debris.

- Train in conditions of limited visibility or at night.
- Interrupt or jam communications.

4-34. As soldier performance levels increase, conditions under which tasks are performed become more demanding while standards remain constant. Soldiers and leaders must execute the planned training, assess performance and retrain until Army standards are met under the most difficult wartime conditions. The same standards must be enforced on a task whether it is performed individually or as part of a larger operation. Soldier and leader training must occur continually and be fully integrated into collective training.

> *Carefully planned, purposeful and effective training...demonstrates concretely the leader's intense concern that the men and the unit receive every possible measure to prepare them to accomplish their mission.*
>
> DA Pam 22-1, *Leadership* (1948)

SAFETY

4-35. Leaders must ensure realistic training is safe; safety awareness protects combat power. Historically, more casualties occur in combat due to accidents than from enemy action. Ensuring that realistic training is safe instills the awareness that will save lives in combat. Conducting realistic training is challenging business. The goal of the chain of command is *not* training first *nor* safety first, but *training safely*. The commander is the safety officer. He is ultimately responsible for unit safety; however, every soldier is responsible for safe training. This includes leaders throughout the chain of command and NCO support channel, not just range safety officers and NCOs, Observer Controllers (OCs) and installation safety officers. NCOs should conduct a risk assessment for every mission they prepare for.

SERGEANT'S TIME TRAINING

4-36. Some training time during the week should be devoted to the small-unit leader (such as a squad leader or a vehicle commander) to train his unit (see Appendix A, Sergeant's Time Training). This enhances readiness and cohesion; it also allows the junior NCO to learn and exercise the Army's training management system at the lowest level. *The key is to train the trainer so that he can train his soldiers.* This requires the NCO to identify essential soldier and small-unit and team tasks (drills) that support unit METL and then the NCO must—

- Assess strengths and weaknesses.
- Formulate a plan to correct deficiencies and sustain strengths.
- Execute the training to standard.

OPPORTUNITY TRAINING

4-37. Opportunity training is the conduct of preselected, prepared instruction on critical tasks that require little explanation. Sometimes called "hip-pocket" training, it is conducted when proficiency has been reached on the scheduled primary training task and time is available. Unscheduled breaks in exercises or assembly area operations, or while waiting for transportation, provide time for opportunity training. Creative, aggressive leaders use this time to sustain the skills of their soldiers and units. For example, an Stinger team crew leader may conduct opportunity training on aircraft identification while waiting to have his crew's MILES re-keyed during a Field Training Exercise (FTX). Good leader books are necessary to select tasks for quality opportunity training.

Drills

4-38. Drills provide small units standard procedures for building strong, aggressive units. A unit's ability to accomplish its mission depends on soldiers, leaders and units executing key actions quickly. All soldiers and their leaders must understand their immediate reaction to enemy contact. They must also understand squad or platoon follow-up actions to maintain momentum and offensive spirit on the battlefield. Drills are limited to situations requiring instantaneous response; therefore, soldiers must execute drills instinctively. This results from continual practice.

4-39. Drills provide standardized actions that link soldier and collective tasks at platoon level and below. At company and above, integration of systems and synchronization demand an analysis of METT-T. Standard Tactics,

_____Training

Techniques and Procedures (TTP) help to speed the decision and action cycle of units above platoon level, but they are not drills. There are two types of drills which apply to *all* type units—battle drills and crew drills.

> **SSG Michael Duda in Desert Storm**
>
> At 1400 on 26 February 1991, a US armor task force consolidated it's position and oriented north on a small desert hill to allow the task force on it's right to catch up. Visibility was less than 1500 meters due to fog, dust and smoke. Spot reports from higher indicated an enemy column of 20 tanks was crossing the brigade front from the east. The trailing task force in the right reported being stationary and over 2 kilometers behind the forward battalion on the left. Spot reports further confirmed the trailing unit's Scouts were in zone and no further north that the forward battalion's positions (vicinity the 39 grid line).
>
> Two T-55s then appeared along a road 2500 meters to the forward unit's front and adjacent to it's right boundary. Upon confirmation, these two tanks were destroyed, one by the task force commander's tank from his right flank vantage point.
>
> A short time later, brigade reemphasized the threat of an enemy tank column from the east and cautioned the commander to be prepared. The trailing battalion reconfirmed it's location south of the 37 grid line, with Scouts vicinity the 39 grid line. During this time the forward battalion continued to have contact and enemy engagements among it's left flank company teams. Then a tank platoon from the right flank of the forward battalion reported two more vehicles vicinity the brightly burning T-55s and moving in a direction consistent with the brigade spot report. The task force commander gave a fire command to that company and initiated a 2700 meter engagement with his own tank. Within moments, his gunner, SSG Michael Duda, exclaimed over the intercom: "Sir, there is something wrong here!" His commander immediately transmitted a cease fire.
>
> Fortunately no one engaged the vehicles. SSG Duda had recognized the "hot" roadwheel thermal signature characteristic of the Bradley Fighting Vehicle (BFV). Quick investigation confirmed this was a misoriented Scout section from the adjacent battalion and almost 4000 meters forward of the reported positions.

4-40. A *battle drill* is a collective action that platoon and smaller units rapidly execute without applying a deliberate decision making process.

- Battle drills require minimal leader orders to accomplish and are standard throughout the Army.
- They continue sequential actions that are vital to success in combat or critical to preserving life.
- They are trained responses to enemy actions or leader's orders.
- Battle drills represent mental steps followed for offensive and defensive actions in training and combat.

4-41. A *crew drill* is a collective action that the crew of a weapon or system must perform to employ the weapon or equipment. This action is a trained response to a given stimulus, such as a leader order or the status of the weapon or equipment. Like a battle drill, a crew drill requires minimal leader orders to accomplish and is standard throughout the Army.

> *"No football coach sends his team out to scrimmage on the first day of practice. He would end up with chaos and a lot of injuries. Instead, he drills the players on individual skills like blocking, tackling and passing. Then he works on collective tasks such as setting up the pocket and pass-release timing. When the players are trained to proficiency in these skills, the coach has them work on plays."*
>
> SSG Rico Johnston

ASSESSMENT

4-42. Leaders use evaluations and other feedback to assess soldier, leader and unit proficiency. The analysis of the information provided through evaluations is key to the commander's assessment.

4-43. The unit assessment is made by the commander. It is based on his firsthand observations and input from all leaders (officer and NCO) and it is the base upon which a training strategy is developed. The unit assessment is—

- Developed using evaluations, reports, leader books, or records.
- A continuous process though formal assessment is usually conducted at the start of planning phases and after major training events.
- Used to set or update unit goals and objectives.
- Influenced by future events; for example, personnel turnover, new equipment fielding, or force structure changes.

4-44. The CSM, 1SGs, platoon sergeants, squad leaders and other key NCOs provide input on squad, section, team and soldier proficiency on essential soldier tasks for the commander's assessment. Leaders also provide input to the commander's assessment of leader proficiency and provide planning recommendations on integrating selected essential leader and soldier tasks into collective mission essential tasks.

ASSESSMENT TOOLS

4-45. NCOs may use a leader book and battle roster to assess section, squad, crew and soldier tasks. Battle rosters provide a way to record key systems crew data. Battle rosters—

- May be maintained formally or informally.
- Are maintained at battalion level and below.

- Track key weapon and support systems, such as tanks, attack helicopters, howitzers, radars, trucks and tube launched, optically tracked, wire-guided (TOW) missiles.
- Track crew data such as stability, manning or qualification status.
- Designate qualified back-up crewmembers.
- Identify soldiers to enable them to train as a designated crew.

4-46. The After-Action Review (AAR) is a structured review process that allows training participants to discover for themselves what happened, why it happened and how it can be done better. AARs—

- Focus on the training objectives — Was the mission accomplished?
- Emphasize meeting Army standards (not who won or lost).
- Encourage soldiers to discover important lessons from the training event.
- Allow a large number of soldiers and leaders (including OPFOR) to participate so those lessons learned can be shared.

4-47. The AAR has four parts:

- Review what was supposed to happen (training plan).
- Establish what happened (to include OPFOR point of view).
- Determine what was right or wrong with what happened.
- Determine how the task should be done differently next time.

AARs are one of the best learning tools we have.... AARs must be a two-way communication between the NCO and the soldiers. They are not lectures.

Center for Army Lessons Learned

TRAINING MEETINGS

4-48. Battalions and companies must conduct training meetings. The focus at battalion and company is in scheduling training based on commanders' assessments. But it is helpful for platoons to conduct training meetings in preparation for company training meetings.

4-49. At the platoon training meeting the focus should be in developing those assessments of individual and crew training levels and communicating these to the higher commander. The platoon meetings also focus on the actual preparation, rehearsal and execution of upcoming training. In any event, all NCOs of the platoon should be there to advise the platoon sergeant and platoon leader of their soldiers' training status and recommend additional training.

4-50. The platoon sergeant ensures that all NCOs are prepared for the meeting. This means everyone being on time and properly equipped. At a minimum,

NCOs need to bring their leader book, paper and pencil/pen, training schedules and a calendar to the meeting.

4-51. Platoons follow an established agenda when executing training meetings. This allows for a quick and efficient meeting as in issuing an Operation Order (OPORD) for a tactical operation. Keeping in mind the three objectives of platoon meetings, a sample agenda is:

- Squad or section training assessments.
- Platoon leader's assessment.
- Preparation for training.
- Future training.
- Command guidance.

4-52. After the company and battalion have had training meetings at their respective levels, important information comes back through the chain of command. A technique to getting this information to all the soldiers is to meet with key leaders and put out information affecting the platoon.

4-53. The NCO's role in training is not only as the trainer of individual soldiers and small units – though clearly that is the primary role. NCOs know the level of training of their soldiers and small units. NCOs must convey this information through the chain of command so training events improve or sustain individual and collective training levels. It is vitally important for NCOs to be involved in assessment and planning of training, as well as preparation and execution.

Leading and training American soldiers – the best job in the world!

Chapter 5

Counseling and Mentorship

We have the best doctrine, the best training and the best equipment in the world – but our people are the Army's greatest resource

	Page
Leader's Responsibility	5-3
Effective Army Counseling Program	5-5
The Counseling Process	5-6
Assess the Plan of Action	5-7
Types of Developmental Counseling	5-7
Event-Oriented Counseling	5-7
Counseling for Specific Instances	5-7
Performance and Professional Growth Counseling	5-10
The Counseling Session	5-13
Mentorship	5-16
Developmental Relationship	5-16
Sustain Mentorship	5-17
NCO Mentorship of Officers	5-18
Mentorship Builds the Future	5-19

For more information on Counseling and Mentorship see FM 6-22 (22-100) *Army Leadership,* Appendix C, Counseling; The Army Leadership Homepage, www leadership.army.mil; and the Army Counseling Homepage, www.counseling.army mil.

For more information on the NCO Evaluation System, see AR 623-205, "Noncommissioned Officer Evaluation Reporting System," 15 May 2002.

For more information on mentorship, see DA PAM 600-XX, "Army Mentorship," TBP.

Counseling and Mentorship

5-1. At the time of the American Revolution, European armies were held together by the most severe discipline. Enlistments in Europe and England were often as long as twenty-five years, pay was very low and punishments were cruel by today's standards. To reduce desertion and motivate troops for battle, the threat of flogging, even death, was held over soldier's heads. Frederick the Great of Prussia set the tone of the period with his view that soldiers should be more afraid of their NCOs then the enemy. From the founding of the Continental Army, the European tradition of harsh discipline was rejected. Friedrich von Steuben, the Army's first trainer and himself a product of the old Prussian tradition, quickly came to understand that it would take more than threats to get American recruits to perform well on the battlefield. General George Washington agreed and together, both leaders recognized that the American soldier was an individual citizen, not an interchangeable commodity. Citizen-soldiers would have to be led, inspired and disciplined by reason, creating the need to counsel.

5-2. To best understand the value of counseling it is best to first understand its definition. Counseling is a type of communication that leaders use to empower soldiers to achieve goals. It is much more than providing feedback or direction. It is communication aimed at developing a soldier's ability to achieve individual and unit goals. Soldiers want to be counseled and will respond to counseling because they want to know what it takes to be successful in today's Army. Regardless of your leadership position, your soldiers see you as successful simply because you have achieved the level they are striving to accomplish. Leaders must provide each of their soldiers with the best possible road map to success. Today's leadership doctrine incorporates this definition in subordinate-centered communication, which leads to the achievement of individual and unit goals.

LEADER'S RESPONSIBILITY

5-3. Today's Army demands effective counseling. Due to the complexity of equipment, diversity of personnel and organizational structure, we have unique challenges. To overcome these problems, a leader has talent, experience and the desire to succeed. Leaders help soldiers solve their problems by guiding them to a workable solution through effective counseling. Counseling is so important it should be on the training schedule to ensure sufficient time is available to do it.

5-4. The Army's values of Loyalty, Duty and Selfless Service require us to counsel. The Army's values of Honor, Integrity and Personal Courage also require us to give straightforward feedback and the Army's value of Respect requires us to find the best way to communicate that feedback.

5-5. Leaders conduct counseling to develop soldiers to achieve personal, professional development and organizational goals, and to prepare them for increased responsibilities. Leaders are responsible for developing their soldiers. Unit readiness and mission accomplishment depend on every member's ability to perform to established standards. Supervisors must develop their subordinates through teaching, coaching and counseling. Leaders coach soldiers the same way any sports coach improves their team: by identifying weaknesses, setting goals, developing and implementing a plan of action and providing oversight and motivation throughout the process. To be effective coaches, leaders must thoroughly understand the strengths, weaknesses and professional goals of their soldiers.

> *"In developmental counseling, it's a matter of sitting the soldier down and telling him not only how well he did over the last thirty days, but also of telling the soldier how he or she can improve their performance and then looking deeper down the road."*

CSM Anthony Williams

5-6. Leaders counsel because it is their duty and the primary tool in developing future leaders. For their counseling to be effective they must be honest and have the personal courage to give straightforward feedback. Through respect for the individual, leaders find the best way to communicate that guidance. Senior NCOs should develop the counseling skills of their subordinate leaders. One way to do this is for the senior NCO to sit in on a counseling session, perhaps a reception and integration counseling, and then do an AAR with the junior NCO.

- Purpose: Clearly define the purpose of the counseling.
- Flexibility: Fit the counseling style to the character of each soldier and to the relationship desired.
- Respect: View soldiers as unique, complex individuals, each with their own sets of values, beliefs and attitudes.
- Communication: Establish open, two-way communication with soldiers using spoken language, nonverbal actions, gestures and body language. Effective counselors listen more than they speak.
- Support: Encourage soldiers through actions while guiding them through their problems.
- Motivation: Get every soldier to actively participate in counseling and understand its value.

Figure 5-1. Characteristics of Effective Counseling

5-7. Some soldiers may perceive counseling as an adverse action. Effective leaders who counsel properly and regularly can change that perception.

Counseling and Mentorship

Leaders conduct counseling to help soldiers become better members of the team, maintain or improve performance and prepare for the future. No easy answers exist for exactly what to do in all leadership and counseling situations. However, to conduct effective counseling, leaders should develop a counseling style with the characteristics listed in Figure 5-1.

> *"You also must ensure the session is not done in a threatening manner. Nothing will destroy communications faster than if the soldier thinks there will be negative consequences to that conversation."*
>
> CSM Daniel E. Wright

EFFECTIVE ARMY COUNSELING PROGRAM

5-8. Four elements are essential to the creation of an effective counseling program:

- **Education and Training**: Institutional and in units, through mentorship and self-development. The Army must first provide a base line of education to its soldiers to "show what right looks like." The Noncommissioned Officer Education System (NCOES) has the primary responsibility to educate the NCO Corps on counseling. However, NCOES cannot accomplish this alone. Unit NCO Development Programs can and must conduct training workshops to provide that base of education of what right looks like to our junior leaders.

- **Experience**: Learn by doing coupled with guidance from more senior leaders. After initial education and training, all leaders must put their skills to use. NCOs must practice counseling while at the same time receiving guidance and mentoring on how to improve counseling techniques.

- **Continued support from both the Army and leaders**: The Army's Counseling Website (www.counseling.army.mil), FM 6-22 (22-100), Appendix B and C and leaders (through spot checks and random monitoring of counseling sessions) provide the necessary support and critiques that will improve a young leader's counseling skills.

- **Enforcement**: Once NCOs have the tools (both education and support) necessary for quality counseling, leaders must hold them accountable to ensure acceptable counseling standards for both frequency and content. This is accomplished through some type of compliance program on unit inspections.

FM 7-22.7

THE COUNSELING PROCESS

5-9. Effective leaders use the counseling process. It consists of four stages:

- Identify the need for counseling.
- Prepare for counseling.
- Conduct counseling.
- Follow-up.

"Listen to what soldiers have to say- they'll tell you everything if you listen openly. Criticize and they'll clam up. Ask what isn't working about programs even if company statistics indicate that they are running well. Soldier comments often provide insight into ways to improve things to save time and make things more meaningful."

COL David Reaney

| Leaders must demonstrate certain qualities to counsel effectively:
• Respect for soldiers.
• Self and cultural awareness.
• Credibility.
• Empathy.
Leaders must possess certain counseling skills:
• Active listening.
• Responding.
• Questioning.
Effective leaders avoid common counseling mistakes. Leaders should avoid the influence of:
• Personal bias.
• Rash judgments.
• Stereotyping.
• The loss of emotional control.
• Inflexible methods of counseling.
• Improper follow-up. | The Counseling Process:
1. Identify the need for counseling.
2. Prepare for counseling:
• Select a suitable place.
• Schedule the time.
• Notify the counselee well in advance.
• Organize information.
• Outline the components of the counseling session.
• Plan counseling strategy.
• Establish the right atmosphere.
3. Conduct the counseling session:
• Open the session.
• Discuss the issue.
• Develop a plan of action (to include the leader's responsibilities).
• Record and Close the session.
4. Follow-up.
• Support Plan of Action Implementation.
• Assess Plan of Action. |

Figure 5-2. Major Aspects of Counseling Process

ASSESS THE PLAN OF ACTION

5-10. The purpose of counseling is to develop soldiers who are better able to achieve personal, professional and organizational goals. During the assessment, review the plan of action with the soldier to determine if the desired results were achieved. The leader and soldier should schedule future follow-up counseling sessions. Figure 5-2 summarizes the major aspects of the counseling process. Additional information on counseling is in Appendix C of FM 6-22 (22-100) and on the Army Counseling Homepage (www.counseling.army.mil).

> *"Nothing will ever replace one person looking another in the eyes and telling the soldier his strengths and weaknesses. [Counseling] charts a path to success and diverts soldiers from heading down the wrong road."*
>
> SGM Randolph S. Hollingsworth

TYPES OF DEVELOPMENTAL COUNSELING

5-11. You can often categorize developmental counseling based on the topic of the session. The two major categories of counseling are event-oriented and performance and professional growth.

EVENT-ORIENTED COUNSELING

5-12. Event-oriented counseling involves a specific event or situation. It may precede events, such as going to a promotion board or attending a school; or it may follow events, such as a noteworthy duty performance, a problem with performance or mission accomplishment, or a personal problem. Examples of event-oriented counseling include, but are not limited to these types:

- Specific instances of superior or substandard performance.
- Reception and integration counseling.
- Crisis counseling.
- Referral counseling.
- Promotion counseling.
- Separation counseling.

COUNSELING FOR SPECIFIC INSTANCES

5-13. Sometimes counseling is tied to specific instances of superior or substandard duty performance. For example, you tell your soldier whether or not the performance met the standard and what the soldier did right or wrong. The key to successful counseling for specific performance is to conduct the counseling session as close to the time of the event as possible.

FM 7-22.7

5-14. When counseling a soldier for specific performance take the following actions:

- Tell the soldier the purpose of the counseling, what was expected and how they failed to meet the standard.
- Address the specific unacceptable behavior or action, not the person's character.
- Tell the soldier the effect of the performance on the rest of the unit.
- Actively listen to the soldier's response.
- Remain unemotional.
- Teach the soldier how to meet the standard.
- Be prepared to do some personal counseling since the lack of performance may be related to or the result of a personal problem.
- Explain to the soldier what will be done to improve performance (plan of action). Identify your responsibilities in implementing the plan of action.
- Continue to assess and follow-up on the soldier's progress. Adjust the plan of action as necessary.

Reception and Integration Counseling

5-15. Leaders must counsel new team members when they report in. Reception and integration counseling serves two purposes: First, it identifies and helps fix any problems or concerns that new members have, especially any issues resulting from the new duty assignment. Second, it lets them know the unit standards and how they fit into the team. Reception and integration counseling starts the team building process and lets the soldier know the leadership cares. Reception and integration counseling clarifies job titles and it sends the message that the chain of command cares. Reception and integration counseling should begin immediately upon arrival so new team members can quickly become integrated into the organization. Figure 5-3 gives some possible discussion points.

_____ **Counseling and Mentorship**

- Unit standards.
- Chain of command.
- NCO support channel (who and how used).
- On and off duty conduct.
- Personnel/personal affairs/initial clothing issue.
- Unit history, organization and mission.
- Soldier programs within the unit, such as soldier of the month/quarter/year and Audie Murphy and Sergeant Morales Board.
- Off limits and danger areas.
- Functions and locations of support activities.
- On and off post recreational, educational, cultural and historical opportunities.
- Foreign nation or host nation orientation.
- Other areas the individual should be aware of, as determined by the rater.

Figure 5-3. Reception and Integration Counseling Points

Crisis Counseling

5-16. You may conduct crisis counseling to get a soldier through the initial shock after receiving negative news, such as notification of the death of a loved one. You help the soldier by listening and providing assistance, as appropriate. Assistance may include referring the soldier to a support activity or coordinating external agency support. Crisis counseling focuses on the soldier's immediate, short-term needs.

Referral Counseling

5-17. Referral counseling helps soldiers work through a personal situation and may follow crisis counseling. Referral counseling also acts as preventative counseling before the situation becomes a problem. Usually, the leader assists the soldier in identifying the problem.

5-18. Outside agencies can help leaders resolve problems. Although it is generally in an individual's best interest to seek help first from his first line leader, leaders must always respect an individual's right to contact these agencies on their own. Leaders can refer the soldier to the appropriate resource, such as Army Community Services, a Chaplain, or a substance abuse counselor. Additional information on support activities can be found in Appendix B, Army Programs or in FM 6-22 (22-100), Appendix C.

FM 7-22.7

> *[Helping] soldiers cope with personal problems...means more than referring the soldier to another person- the chaplain, a doctor, or counselor. Until the problem is resolved, you have a soldier with a problem in your unit, so it's your problem.... Let your soldiers know what you're doing to help them solve their problems.*
>
> FM 22-600-20, *The Army Noncommissioned Officer Guide*, 1980

Promotion Counseling

5-19. Commanders or their designated representatives must conduct promotion counseling for all specialists, corporals and sergeants who are eligible for advancement without waiver, but are not recommended for promotion to the next higher grade. Army regulations require that soldiers within this category receive initial (event-oriented) counseling when they attain full eligibility and then periodic (performance and personal growth) counseling at least quarterly.

Adverse Separation Counseling

5-20. Adverse separation counseling may involve informing the soldier of the administrative actions available to the commander in the event substandard performance continues and of the consequences associated with those administrative actions. (See AR 635-200, Chapter 1, paragraph 1-16 and Chapter 17.)

5-21. Developmental counseling may not apply when a soldier has engaged in more serious acts of misconduct. In those situations, the leader should refer the matter to the commander and the servicing staff judge advocate's office. When the leader's rehabilitative efforts fail, counseling with a view towards separation fills an administrative prerequisite to many administrative discharges and serves as a final warning to the soldier to improve performance or face discharge. In many cases, it may be beneficial to involve the chain of command as soon as you determine that adverse separation counseling might be required. The first sergeant or commander should inform the soldier of the notification requirements outlined in AR 635-200.

PERFORMANCE AND PROFESSIONAL GROWTH COUNSELING

Performance Counseling

5-22. During performance counseling, the leader conducts a review of the soldier's duty performance during the previous quarter. The leader and soldier jointly establish performance objectives and standards for the next quarter. Rather than dwelling on the past, leaders should focus the session on the soldier's strengths, areas needing improvement and potential.

_____ **Counseling and Mentorship**

Performance counseling informs soldiers about their jobs and the expected performance standards and provides feedback on actual performance -- the best counseling is always looking forward. It does not dwell on the past and what was done, rather on the future and what can be done better.

DA Pam 623-205, "The NCO Evaluation Reporting System 'In Brief,'" 1988

5-23. Performance counseling is required for noncommissioned officers; mandatory, face-to-face performance counseling between the rater and the rated NCO is required under the NCOER system.

5-24. Performance counseling at the beginning of and during the evaluation period facilitates a soldier's involvement in the evaluation process. Performance counseling communicates standards and is an opportunity for leaders to establish and clarify the expected values, attributes, skills and actions.

5-25. As an Army leader, you must ensure you've tied your expectations to performance objectives and appropriate standards. **You must establish standards that your soldiers can work towards and must teach them how to achieve those standards if they are to develop.**

The NCO Evaluation Report

5-26. The Noncommissioned Officer Evaluation Reporting System (NCOERS) is designed to –

- Strengthen the ability of the NCO Corps to meet the professional challenges of the future through the indoctrination of Army values and basic NCO responsibilities. The continued use of Army values and NCO responsibilities as evaluation criteria provides and reinforces a professional focus for the rating chain's view of performance. Over time, this results in acceptance of the values and NCO responsibilities, better performance and a stronger NCO Corps.

- Ensure the selection of the best qualified noncommissioned officers to serve in positions of increasing responsibility by providing rating chain view of performance/potential for use in centralized selection, assignment and other Enlisted Personnel Management System (EPMS) decisions. The information in evaluation reports, the Army's needs and the individual NCO's qualifications are used together as a basis for such personnel actions as school selection, promotion, assignment, military occupational specialty (MOS) classification, command sergeant major (CSM) designation and qualitative management.

- Contribute to Army-wide improved performance and professional development by increased emphasis on performance counseling. Evaluation reports provide the NCO formal recognition for performance of duty, measurement of professional values and personal traits and along with the NCO Counseling Checklist/Records are the basis for performance counseling

FM 7-22.7

by rating officials. Senior/subordinate communication is necessary to maintain high professional standards and is key to an effective evaluation system.

5-27. To ensure that sound personnel management decisions can be made and that an NCO's potential can be fully developed, evaluation reports must be accurate and complete. Each report must be a thoughtful, fair appraisal of an NCO's ability and potential. Reports that are incomplete or fail to provide a realistic and objective evaluation make personnel management decisions difficult.

5-28. A single report should not, by itself, determine an NCO's career. An appraisal philosophy that recognizes continuous professional development and growth (rather than one that demands immediate, uncompromising perfection) best serves the Army and the NCO.

Professional Growth Counseling

5-29. Professional growth counseling is subordinate-centered communication that outlines actions necessary for soldiers to achieve individual and organizational goals and objectives. It is imperative for all leaders to conduct professional growth counseling with their soldiers to develop the leaders of tomorrow.

5-30. Professional growth counseling begins an initial counseling within 30 days of arrival. Additional counseling occurs **quarterly thereafter with an assessment at a minimum of once a month**. Counseling is a continuous process. Reception/Integration/Initial counseling must include goals/expectations for most current quarter along with long term goals and expectations.

5-31. During the counseling session a review is conducted jointly by the leader and soldier to identify and discuss the soldier's strengths/weaknesses and to create a plan of action to build upon strengths and overcome weaknesses. The leader must encourage, remain objective/positive, assist the soldier help himself and focus more towards the future. This future-oriented approach establishes short and long-term goals and objectives.

5-32. FM 6-22 (22-100), Appendix B, provides the necessary tools for the soldier to do a self-assessment based on performance indicators outlined in the leadership dimension. This self-assessment will assist soldiers in identifying their weaknesses and strengths and provide a means of improving their leadership abilities/skills. All leaders should use the performance indicators in FM 6-22 (22-100), Appendix B, as an assessment tool when counseling their

_____ **Counseling and Mentorship**

soldiers. This will assist them in providing specific, precise and objective guidance to their soldiers.

THE COUNSELING SESSION

This is an example of a Performance/Professional Growth counseling session presented in four parts. It shows disagreement between the leader and led on the leadership assessment. This makes the counseling session difficult for both at first (each is a little defensive). SFC Lang has difficulty getting SSG Rovero to do an honest self-appraisal of his performance. The strategy in this situation is to provide SSG Rovero with clear examples of his leader behavior along with the adverse effects it is having on the soldiers and the unit.

SFC LANG: Come in.

SSG ROVERO: Sorry I'm late, SFC Lang. I got tied up on a job that's been running late.

SFC LANG: Have a seat SSG Rovero and lets get started. Do you have your self-assessment with you? *[This reinforces the expectation that all leaders will prepare a self-assessment prior to developmental counseling. This also is a good technique to try in order to get the subordinate leader to start with most of the talking]*

SSG ROVERO: I have it here somewhere. Yes here it is. You know, SFC Lang, after I finished reading my self-assessment, I realized, hey, I'm pretty good!

SFC LANG: You want to know the truth? You are pretty good, but... *[Here, the leader is trying to reinforce and recognize good performance even though it's clear the leader is not satisfied with some other aspects of the subordinate leader's performance]*

SSG ROVERO: Thanks. But?

SFC LANG: Well, like you said; you always seem to be running late on jobs.

SSG ROVERO: Well, some of the guys have been goofing off lately and I just haven't been able to get them back in line yet, that's all. *[There can be a tendency to place blame or identify causal factors that may or may not be beyond the control of the subordinate leader]*

SFC LANG: Well that's why we're here.

SSG ROVERO: What do you mean? *[The leader can expect that some subordinates will be pretty defensive when it comes to leadership assessment. It will be viewed by some as threatening]*

SFC LANG: I thought we went over this last week when we set up this meeting. What'd I say then?

SSG ROVERO: Something about assessing my leadership strengths; areas I can improve in...

SFC LANG: That's part of it. The focus is on developing your leadership.

SSG ROVERO: That's funny, Sergeant. I was a squared away NCO until I got here. Now, all of a sudden I've got all this stuff to improve on. *[Initially, leaders can expect to have many soldiers who have never received feedback on their leadership. As developmental counseling becomes ingrained in the Army, more*

FM 7-22.7

soldiers will be comfortable and familiar with leadership assessment and development]

SFC LANG: Well, leadership is a bigger part of your job now. Leadership responsibilities increase as you move up in the ranks. You've got a lot of attributes in your favor. Like I said, you have very good technical skills, but... *[Again, the leader reinforces the good performance while still trying to get the subordinate leader to admit and 'own up' to the shortcomings that need improvement]*

SSG ROVERO: I run a good shop. Our supply room is always stocked – nobody ever has to borrow a tool from another company. And I go to bat for my soldiers. Like when Hennessey needed time to take care of some family business. I helped him with that. Right? Isn't that leadership?

SFC LANG: Yes, but that's not the whole story... *[SFC Lang has already mentioned she has concerns with SSG Rovero's leadership. She wants SSG Rovero to tell his side of the story and complete his self-assessment. Does he think everything is going well?]*

SSG ROVERO: Well, okay, maybe things in the shop aren't going as smoothly as they should be. And maybe it is my fault, but...

SSG Rovero realizes he could make some improvements in some areas.

SFC LANG: The way I see it, you act like you're still a mechanic instead of a supervisor. Every time I walk through the bays you're under some vehicle turning wrenches. But while you're doing that, who's making sure all the jobs in the shop are getting done? Sometimes these young mechanics we've got are just spinning their wheels. Maybe if you spent more time making the rounds and checking up on each job, we'd have a better OR rate. Plus we might be able to get out of here at a decent hour. *[SFC Lang knew this would probably*

5-14

_____ **Counseling and Mentorship**

be a sore spot with SSG Rovero. But, this is what the supervisor is observing along with the general effect it is having on soldiers and the unit]
SSG ROVERO: I don't think that is what's really happening.
SFC LANG: OK, I've got several observations here; let's take yesterday for example. We had three HMMWVs deadlined with electrical problems. Those new soldiers, Harris, Jones and Wilson, worked on them all day and still couldn't figure out what was causing the problem. Meanwhile, you're over with another HMMWV changing tires. *[SFC Lang did her homework. Observing and assessing is part of her daily activity around the motor pool. Specific observations of leader behavior along with the effects they are having on individuals, the unit and operational outcomes are key prerequisites to developmental activities]*
SSG ROVERO: Somebody had to do it.
SFC LANG: And are the HWMMVs up? [Links behavior to outcomes]
SSG ROVERO: We're working on it.
SFC LANG: And when did everybody finish and leave last night? *[Again this question links leader behavior to outcomes. SFC Lang asks SSG Rovero rather than tells him the outcome to promote ownership]*
SSG ROVERO: About twenty-one hundred.
SFC LANG: We have to agree on what's happening here.
SSG ROVERO: Maybe you're right, Sergeant. I need to work on my organizational skills. I'm not comfortable walking around with a list of jobs and checking up on people. I'd rather do it myself. *[It appears as though SFC Lang's detailed assessment resulted in SSG Rovero becoming a little more honest with himself. Given that SFC Lang also evaluates SSG Rovero, leaders can expect that soldiers might hesitate to admit to shortcomings]*
SFC LANG: I understand, but leaders have to learn how to assign tasks and supervise. That's the only way our soldier's will learn.
SSG ROVERO: OK, Sergeant.

Once they both agree on the assessment, both SFC Lang and SSG Rovero visibly relax. From this point on, the tone of the counseling session turns visibly positive and developmental as they talk about ways to improve SSG Rovero's performance.

SFC LANG: So what could you do to improve your leadership skills? *[Action plan development is a joint activity. The leader should refrain from prescribing developmental tasks unless the subordinate has no clue what to do or where to begin. Having the soldier identify the developmental task also promotes ownership and additional motivation to follow through]*
SSG ROVERO: I know I need to learn how to delegate tasks. I could prioritize the work that needs to be done and assign jobs based on experience. That way I could spend more time training and supervising my more inexperienced soldiers. *[This reinforces the concept that leaders should solicit the input of their soldiers and peers and include them in the decision-making process]*
SFC LANG: Sounds like you have a good plan. Remember, all your soldiers need your supervision. *[SFC Lang is making a subtle correction here to put a little more structure into this developmental plan.]*
SSG ROVERO: Thanks for your help, Sergeant.

FM 7-22.7 _____

MENTORSHIP

5-33. Mentorship, probably the singular most misunderstood word surrounding counseling and leadership. To best understand mentorship, it is best to first define it. Mentorship is a voluntary, developmental relationship that exists between a person of greater experience and a person of lesser experience. Mentorship is not just a fancy buzzword. It is a proven approach and a valuable tool for NCO leaders.

> *"The experiences of the mentor when shared gives the soldier a comparative view to allow the soldier to develop and grow. The mentor is the sage old owl who has been there and done that and uses the experience to counsel wisely that young soldier."*
>
> CSM A. Frank Lever, III

5-34. Note that no specific action is exclusively "mentoring." In fact, the term "mentoring" is often used to describe a wide array of actions that outside of a mentorship relationship refer to the core of leader development such as counseling, teaching, coaching, role modeling, advising and guiding.

> *To be an effective mentor, you need the experience and wisdom of your years. You also have to care. If you really care about your soldiers, then you will devote the necessary time and attention to guiding them. Mentoring can take place anywhere. It is a key way to lead and to strengthen Army values.*
>
> DA Pam 600-25, "NCO Development Program," 1987

DEVELOPMENTAL RELATIONSHIP

5-35. Mentorship is clearly a developmental relationship and noncommissioned officers have a mandate to develop their soldiers. Given that fact, shouldn't all leader-follower relationships be considered mentorship? Or why confuse the issue by labeling as mentorship what is in the essence, good leadership? Why do we need mentorship? When those mandated leader development actions occur within a mentorship relationship, their potential impact is greatly magnified, both for the individual and for the Army. This increase in development is due primarily because of the high degree of trust and respect that characterizes a mentoring relationship. Simply put good leadership stimulates development; mentorship magnifies that development. See Figure 5-4.

> *"One of the most important responsibilities of a leader is to train, coach and mentor subordinates... Some folks might maintain a relationship with an old mentor throughout their careers and use them as a sounding board and for guidance, but most people will have several mentors over their careers. Keep in mind that a **mentor** is not a substitute for personal research, personal planning, hard work and dedication to service."*
>
> CSM Larry W. Gammon

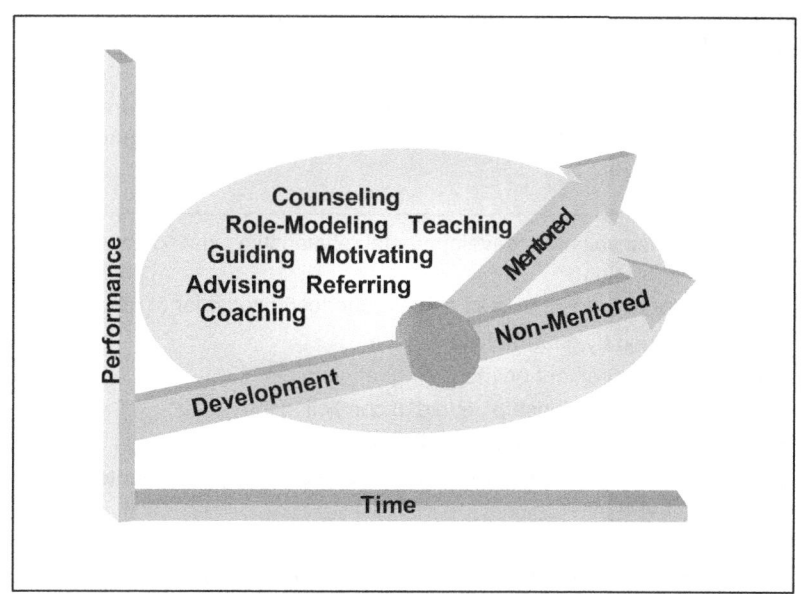

Figure 5-4. Mentorship Development

5-36. Mentorship can and will augment the natural development that occurs in leadership, but it is not necessary or practical in all leader-follower relationships. Soldiers will still develop if they are not mentored, but mentorship can be a key element in the development of soldiers, contributing to their greater well-being. We all have experience to give if we have the heart, the spirit and the caring attitude to share these experiences and the lessons we derive from them. Mentoring is simply giving of your knowledge to other people. To be an effective mentor, all you need is experience and the wisdom of your years and one other vital quality — *you have to care!*

> *"Soldiers want to know what's going on. They don't want to reinvent the wheel to address problems that someone else has already solved."*
>
> CSM Cynthia A. Pritchett

SUSTAIN MENTORSHIP

5-37. Mentorship is demanding business, but the future of the Army depends on the trained and effective leaders whom you leave behind. Sometimes it requires you to set priorities, to balance short-term readiness with long-term leader development. The commitment to mentoring future leaders may require you to take risks. It requires you to give soldiers the opportunity to learn and develop them while using your experience to guide them without micromanaging. Mentoring will lead your soldiers to successes that build their confidence and skills for the future. The key to mentorship in the US Army is

FM 7-22.7

that it is a sustained relationship and may last through the entire career of a young soldier and even into retirement.

5-38. While not a formal, mandated program like counseling, mentorship does have some very distinct characteristics that we can use as a guide for our mentoring. See Figure 5-5.

- Personal, voluntary developmental relationship existing between soldiers.
- Mentor is a close, trusted and experienced counselor or guide.
- Not bound by geographical location.
- Mutual agreement on mentoring relationship.
- Mentoring relationship devoid of conflicting interests.
- Common professional interests.
- Enduring relationship, frequency based on need, not predetermined event or time.
- Shared Army Values.
- Soldier may have more than one mentor over time.
- Two-way communications.
- Mentor must be willing to share professional knowledge, training and experience in a trusted and respected atmosphere.
- Mentor maintains confidentiality and trust.
- Sincere caring on part of the mentor.
- Relationship may be initiated by superior, peer, or subordinate.
- Can cross military, civilian, active or retired lines.

Figure 5-5. Mentorship Characteristics

"Soldiers can solve 98 percent of their problems by just talking to someone about them. All you have to do is listen."

SMA William G. Bainbridge

NCO MENTORSHIP OF OFFICERS

5-39. Senior NCOs have a great deal of experience that is valuable to officers. An officer who has an NCO as a mentor is taking advantage of that experience and also of the unique perspective NCOs develop in leadership, training and professionalism. Even very senior officers seek trusted NCOs' advice and counsel. A mentorship relationship that is unique in the Army and the NCO Corps is the relationship between a platoon sergeant and his young platoon leader. Especially in their early years, young officers need to be paired with senior experienced NCOs. The relationship that frequently comes from this experience tends to be instrumental in the young officers' development. Young

_____ **Counseling and Mentorship**

officers may forget a lot of things about their time in the military, but they will never forget, good or bad, their first platoon sergeant.

MENTORSHIP BUILDS THE FUTURE

5-40. Mentorship offers unparalleled opportunities to build a better Army. If you are a noncommissioned officer and are not mentoring several promising young leaders, you are missing an important opportunity to contribute to the Army's future. Mentorship is the single, easiest way to develop young leaders. But to do so, the mentor must be willing to commit the time and energy necessary to do it right and to set the conditions for success so young leaders will seek him out to be their mentor.

> *"Becoming a mentor should not be a hasty endeavor. It is not a part-time job. It is an intense relationship between teacher and student. The process requires time and caring. Effective mentors are totally committed to spending the necessary time and attention it takes to share values, attitudes and beliefs. This includes helping a soldier make career decisions and providing support and encouragement that allow leaders to grow."*
>
> CSM Christine E. Seitzinger

Near the end of the session, SSG Rovero starts taking charge of his action plan – identifying, without SFC Lang's assistance, things he can do to improve his leadership. As the session closes, there is a renewed air of respect and understanding between SFC Lang and SSG Rovero.

FM 7-22.7

SFC LANG: Why don't you read back to me what you've got. *[As developmental sessions come to a close, it is important to review tasks and confirm what was said earlier in the session]*
SSG ROVERO: Okay. *[Making notes to himself.]* "Conduct an AAR with the maintenance section; observe Sergeant Leroy supervising maintenance operations."
SFC LANG: Those should both work to improve Executing. *[SFC Lang reinforces the leadership doctrinal framework by listing developmental tasks IAW with the value, attribute, skill and/or action it is designed to improve]*
SSG ROVERO: One I just thought of, "develop a daily plan for supervising maintenance operations." I think if I just sat down each morning and split up the jobs better, plus figure out where I'm needed most... *[This is an ideal outcome to be sought after in developmental counseling — the subordinate leader coming up with and identifying developmental tasks. Also note the total number of tasks identified. A few clearly defined tasks with high potential for improvement and are better than numerous, ill-defined tasks with questionable outcomes]*
SFC LANG: Sounds good. OR rate is bound to go up. And just think of what this is going to do to everybody's motivation around here – getting home at a decent hour. And I'll let Sergeant LeRoy know you're coming over to have a look at his maintenance operations. *[Again, the action plan may very well require action on the part of the leader, not just the subordinate leader. At a minimum the leader is going to have to plan and allocate time to get out and make subsequent observations of the leader to assess whether or not improvement is being made and perhaps conduct some on-the-spot coaching]*. Well, Sergeant, we've had some pretty straight talk here on things that need to improve. And don't forget you've got a lot going for you. Best technical skill I've seen. Keep up the good work. *[Action plans are also about sustaining the 'good stuff.' In closing the session, SFC Lang is conscience of the need to reinforce and communicate what SSG Rovero is doing well]*
SSG ROVERO: Appreciate that, SFC Lang.

5-41. During the counseling, the leader and soldier conduct a review to identify and discuss the soldier's strengths and weaknesses and create a plan of action to build upon strengths and overcome weaknesses. This counseling is not normally event-driven. The discussion may include opportunities for civilian or military schooling, future duty assignments, special programs and reenlistment options. Every person's needs are different and leaders must apply specific courses of action tailored to each soldier.

Appendix A

Sergeant's Time Training

	Page
Why it is	A-1
What it is	A-1
Who conducts STT	A-2
What Training Occurs During STT	A-2
NCO Responsibilities	A-2
What it is Not	A-3
A Technique	A-3

WHY IT IS

A-1. NCOs are the primary trainers of our soldiers. Sergeant's Time Training (STT) affords a prime opportunity for developing our first line leaders while they gain confidence of their soldiers. Active Component commanders should institute STT as a regular part of the units training program. This will allow NCOs to train certain tasks to their soldiers in a small group environment. Tasks must crosswalk all the way to the Battalion Mission Essential Task List (METL) and commanders must direct their focus on the Quarterly Training Guidance.

> *"[Sergeant's Time Training] is where you bring it all together. NCOs plan it, they execute it, they evaluate it and they decide whether or not retraining is warranted. One day a week for five continuous hours NCOs have all their soldiers mandated to be present at training."*
>
> GEN Eric K. Shinseki

A-2. STT is an excellent tool in preparing our soldiers to fight and win our Nation's wars in combat operations. Commanders should set this time aside exclusively for the NCO leadership to train their soldiers (squads, sections, crews and teams) on METL related tasks under realistic as possible conditions. In combat, it will be the first line leaders that ensure steady and precise execution by our soldiers. NCOs and their soldiers must have the confidence that their unit can accomplish essential combat skills to standard. From STT soldiers develop greater confidence in their first line leaders and those leaders gain more confidence in themselves. Sergeant's Time Training is our best opportunity to build that leadership. Therefore, we need to use the time wisely.

WHAT IT IS

A-3. Sergeant's Time Training is hands-on, practical training for soldiers given by their NCOs. It provides our NCOs with resources and the authority to

FM 7-22.7

bring training publications or Technical Manuals to life and to develop the trust between leader and led to ensure success in combat. In the Active Component, the chain of command and NCO support channel support this vital training event by scheduling five uninterrupted hours of STT each week, usually conducted on Thursday mornings from 0700 – 1200 hours. In the Reserve Component, STT may be difficult to accomplish during a typical Unit Training Assembly or even during Annual Training. But even RC units should plan and conduct STT after mobilization.

WHO CONDUCTS STT

A-4. First line leaders are the primary trainers during STT and should strive for 100% of their soldier's present for training. Platoon sergeants assist in the preparation and execution of the training. Officers provide the METL and resources (time, personnel and equipment) to evaluate training and provide feedback to commanders. Senior NCOs should protect this program against distractions and provide leadership and guidance as necessary to the first line leader. They must train their soldiers to standard (not to time) oriented on specific tasks to provide the important one-on-one exchange between NCO leaders and their soldiers.

WHAT TRAINING OCCURS DURING STT

A-5. NCOs conduct a training assessment and recommend what MOS soldier task or crew and squad collective training they need to conduct during STT. Topics are based on the small unit leader's assessment of training areas that need special attention. The small unit leader recommends the subjects for Sergeant's Time Training at unit training meetings so that the training can be identified, resourced and rehearsed prior to execution. The commander puts this training on the training schedule four to six weeks prior to execution. Schedule resources for the training four weeks before the training.

NCO RESPONSIBILITIES

A-6. Command sergeants major will monitor and provide detailed guidance for STT, provide technical expertise, check training to ensure standards are established and maintained and advise both commanders and first sergeants on their program. Preparation is the key to a successful training session and program.

A-7. First sergeants will ensure that NCOs scheduled to conduct training do a risk assessment and rehearse the class prior to training their soldiers.

A-8. Sergeant's Time Training may be used to train soldiers in a low-density MOS by consolidating soldiers across battalion / brigade and other organizations. The senior NCO in a low-density MOS conducts training for other soldiers holding that MOS even if he doesn't supervise the soldiers

_____ **Sergeant's Time Training**

directly. Commanders and their NCOs decide on the frequency of low-density MOS training but it usually occurs once or twice a month. An example for low-density MOS training is that for supply clerks in a Transportation Battalion. Even for low-density MOS training, the Battalion CSM and each first sergeant is responsible for implementation of the program.

WHAT IT IS NOT

A-9. Sergeant's Time Training is not company or battery time, nor is it a "round robin" training event. Company / battery annual mandatory training, physical training, inventories, weapons and routine maintenance should not occur during this time. STT should be hands on training, involving all soldiers and that builds proficiency in essential warfighting tasks. Do not have platoon sergeants as instructors; they should be checking training and ensuring it is conducted to standard. Your unit should conduct STT regularly except during extraordinary events like post-operations maintenance or during field training exercises. You may have minimum essential phone watch, CQs and guards.

A TECHNIQUE

A-10. While many units have their own, unique way of conducting STT, some aspects are universal. The training will be standard oriented and not time oriented. Continue training on a task until soldiers are proficient in that task, that is, they receive a "GO" or perform the task to standard. You should use the training management cycle when developing and executing your STT. Use hands-on-training as much as possible. All first line supervisors will maintain a file with the task, conditions and standards for each task and record each soldier's proficiency in those tasks.

A-11. Supervisors maintain a Sergeant's Time Training Book with a list of collective and individual tasks their squad/section/team/crew must be proficient in to support their Battery/Company METL. Rate each task as "T" (trained), "P" (needs practice), or "U" (untrained). The full text of these tasks is in the appropriate MTP. This information is essential input for training assessments and training meetings.

A-12. Sergeant's Time Training is an NCO led program. The first line supervisor must be able to justify to the chain of command why he is training a selected task, such as it was a training weakness during the last FTX. You should not train on a "T" task before a "U" task. If a supervisor can justify his training plan, then the training is probably worthwhile and necessary. For example, units that are not Table VIII qualified must train on those tasks until qualified. This would be an example of a collective task that is a "U."

A-13. Have written **task, conditions and standards** prepared for each training event. Post the task, condition and standards so that any visitor that enters the training site knows what task is you are training and who the instructor is conducting the class. Additionally, designate a secondary instructor so the supervisor on site can brief any visitors.

A-14. At the end of Sergeant's Time Training, the supervisor will assess the training conducted and make recommendations for future training. If the task could not be trained to standard, then the supervisor should reschedule the same task for a future Sergeant's Time. Leaders should annotate the results of the STT in their leader books.

A-15. The **Sergeant's Time Training Book** should contain as a minimum:
- Unit METL with all collective tasks supporting each METL task and each individual task supporting each collective task.
- Critical individual tasks, must be accomplished in order to make the collective task work, must be identified.
- Lesson plan.
- A soldier sign-in accountability status sheet roster.
- A visitor sign-in roster.
- Risk assessment checklist, completed.
- The Sergeant's Time Training Book must be at your site location at all times during training.

A-16. Sergeant's Time Training **equipment required** at the training location includes:
- All soldiers are in the same uniform IAW, your unit's SOP.
- Operational equipment to train on (tank, aiming circle, Launcher/Loader, etc.)
- Required reference materials.
- Butcher board and writing instruments.
- Visual training aids required.

A-17. An **Example** Sergeant's Time Training Timeline:
- 0700 - 1130 instruction / hands-on test/ AAR after each task.
- 1130 - 1200 final AAR, return to unit area.

A-18. You as an NCO and a leader are responsible for conducting Sergeant's Time Training to standard and not to time. Your soldiers will rely on you to provide them with realistic training conducted in a field environment. Don't disappoint your soldiers by not being prepared and your STT won't be a waste of their time. This is your chance to teach your soldiers those important tasks. Set the example.

Appendix B

Army Programs

	Page
Transition Assistance	B-1
Equal Opportunity	B-2
Equal Employment Opportunity	B-2
Education	B-2
Army Substance Abuse Program	B-3
Army Emergency Relief	B-4
Quality of Life Programs	B-4
Army Sponsorship Program	B-4
Better Opportunities For Single Soldiers (BOSS)	B-5
American Red Cross	B-5
Army Community Service (ACS)	B-6
Morale, Welfare and Recreation	B-7
Army Family Action Plan	B-7
Family Readiness Programs	B-7

B-1. This appendix includes aspects of military programs that include human resources management, education, community and family support programs. The Army has entered into a partnership with its soldiers and families to make available programs and services needed. These are to provide a quality of life that is equal to that of their fellow Americans. Personnel and community activities reach all components of the America's Army family. These activities cover a broad spectrum of programs and services. They extend from the management of civilian and military personnel to issues related to family programs. Child and youth services, child abuse or neglect and spouse abuse, exceptional family members and relocation and transition assistance are often emotional and routinely demand command attention. The programs directly impact morale, organizational esprit and personal development. As the Army becomes a smaller force, it fosters even greater expectations for continued Quality of Life (QOL) programs.

TRANSITION ASSISTANCE

B-2. The Army Career and Alumni Program (ACAP) serves as the commander's primary agency for developing, coordinating and delivering transition employment services. It supports eligible soldiers, DA Civilians and their families. The ACAP consists of a Transition Assistance Office (TAO) and a job assistance center. The TAO must be the first step in the transition process. The TAO provides individual transition plans, integrates installation services and provides quality control to the transition process. The job assistance center is the contracted installation service provider delivering job search skills and access to a national and local job resource database and career counseling. Through the services of ACAP, the Army shows that it does take care of its own. ACAP provides assistance to individuals leaving active duty as well as DA Civilian employees who are also transitioning to the work force as private citizens. The Army Community Service provides these services on installations that do not have ACAP offices.

EQUAL OPPORTUNITY

B-3. The Equal Opportunity (EO) program formulates, directs and sustains a comprehensive effort to maximize human potential and to ensure fair treatment for all persons based solely on merit, fitness and capability in support of readiness. EO philosophy is based on fairness, justice and equity. Commanders are responsible for sustaining a positive EO climate within their units. Specifically, the goals of the EO program are to-

- Provide EO for military personnel and family members, both on and off post and within the limits of the laws of localities, states and host nations. AR 600-20, Chapter 6 provides further information.
- Create and sustain effective units by eliminating discriminatory behaviors or practices that undermine teamwork, mutual respect, loyalty and shared sacrifice of the men and women of America's Army.

EQUAL EMPLOYMENT OPPORTUNITY

B-4. The Equal Employment Opportunity (EEO) Program has similar goals as the EO Program but is designed to assist and protect the civilians supporting the Army and Department of Defense. It ensures equal opportunity in all aspects of employment for Army civilian employees and applicants for employment. Employment policies and practices in DA will be free from unlawful discrimination based on race, color, religion, sex, age, national origin, or handicap. The basic principle of equal employment opportunity underlies all aspects of the civilian personnel management program in the Army. The implementation of the program allows civilian employees to make complaints when they believe they have been discriminated against. More information is available in AR 690-12 and AR 690-600.

> *"We want our army to be society's model of fair treatment. We want to assure that all soldiers are treated fairly, not because it is necessary but because it is right."*
>
> SMA Silas L. Copeland

EDUCATION

B-5. The Army Continuing Education System (ACES) provides educational programs and services to support the professional and personal development of soldiers, adult family members and DA Civilians. ACES programs help to improve the combat readiness of America's Army by expanding soldier skills, knowledge and aptitudes to produce confident, competent leaders. Education programs and services support the enlistment, retention and transition of soldiers. ACES instills the organizational value of education within the Army. It promotes the professional and personal value of education to the individual soldier. Education centers provide support for all military, civilian and family members through local community colleges and universities.

ARMY SUBSTANCE ABUSE PROGRAM

B-6. The Army Substance Abuse Program (ASAP) is a comprehensive command program providing assistance to active duty and retired service members and their families with substance abuse problems. Command involvement throughout the identification, referral, screening and elevation process is critical. ASAP participation is mandatory for soldiers who are command referred. Refusal to participate constitutes violation of a direct order. Soldiers who fail to participate in or fail to respond successfully to rehabilitation must leave the Army. Soldiers begin rehabilitation through voluntary (self-referral), command referrals, biochemical, medical and investigation and apprehension. Commanders must refer all soldiers for an evaluation if they suspect a problem may exist. This includes knowledge that a soldier was convicted of Driving While Intoxicated (DWI) off post or out of state. Referral is not punishment and commanders should not wait until the matter is resolved in court.

B-7. An ASAP counselor will conduct an initial screening evaluation interview as soon as possible with any soldier being referred to the ASAP and will recommend one or more of the following:

- Counseling by the unit commander.
- Referral to another agency such as ACS or Mental Health.
- No ASAP service required.
- Enrollment in ASAP rehabilitation.

B-8. The commander's attitude and involvement are critical in the rehabilitation process. The commander must ensure that soldiers suspected of having substance abuse problems have the chance for evaluation and treatment. The objectives of rehabilitation are to return the soldier to full duty as soon as possible and identify those who cannot be rehabilitated. Rehabilitation of substance abusers is a command responsibility. For more information see AR 600-85.

ARMY EMERGENCY RELIEF

B-9. The Army Emergency Relief (AER) is a non-profit organization. It is dedicated to providing assistance to –

- Active duty soldiers and their dependents.
- Soldiers of the Army National Guard and US Army, Reserve on active duty for more than 30 days and their dependents.
- Retirees and their dependents.
- Surviving spouses and orphans of soldiers who died while on active duty or after they retired.

B-10. AER can usually help with emergency needs for: rent, utilities (not including phone or cable television), food, emergency travel, emergency POV repair, up front funeral expenses of parents, spouse or child and emergency medical or dental expenses. AER cannot help with: nonessential needs, ordinary leave or vacation, fines or legal expenses, debt payments, home purchases or improvements, purchase, rental, or lease of a vehicle, funds to cover bad checks and marriage or divorce.

B-11. Active duty soldiers who need assistance may get the appropriate form (DA 1103) at their unit obtain the commander's authorization. Unaccompanied dependents, surviving spouses or orphans, retirees and others not assigned to or under control of your installation may get forms at the AER office. All applicants need their military ID card and substantiating documents (i.e., car repair estimate, rental contract, etc.). Army members can also receive assistance at any Navy Relief, Air Force Aid Society or Coast Guard Mutual Assistance Office. If not near a military installation, soldiers can receive assistance through the American Red Cross. For more information see AR 930-4.

QUALITY OF LIFE PROGRAMS

B-12. Quality of life (QOL) is dedicated to the precept that the Army's number one operational resource must be taken care of. A number of programs improve Army Quality of Life.

ARMY SPONSORSHIP PROGRAM

B-13. The Army Sponsorship Program provides the structure for units to welcome and help prepare soldiers for their new duty station in advance of their actual arrival. Not only does the program help a soldier learn about his new assignment but the sponsor (appointed by the commander to assist the incoming soldier) may also send housing or local schools information to the incoming soldier. The sponsor is the key to helping the new soldier and his family get comfortably settled as quickly as possible, thereby putting his mind at rest so he can concentrate on his military duties as soon as possible. Sponsorship programs include the following:

- In-Sponsorship.
- Out-Sponsorship.
- Reactionary Sponsorship.
- Rear Detachment Sponsorship.
- New Manning Systems.
- Unit Sponsorship.

For more information on Army Sponsorship see AR 600-8-8 and your unit Sponsorship Program proponent.

BETTER OPPORTUNITIES FOR SINGLE SOLDIERS (BOSS)

B-14. Better Opportunities for Single Soldiers (BOSS) is a program that supports the overall quality of single soldier's lives. BOSS identifies well-being issues and concerns by recommending improvements through the chain of command. BOSS encourages and assists single soldiers in identifying and planning for recreational and leisure activities. Additionally, it gives single soldiers the opportunity to participate in and contribute to their respective communities. The Three Pillars of BOSS are the following:

- **Recreation**: Activities may be planned by the BOSS committee or by the BOSS committee working in conjunction with other Morale, Welfare and Recreation activities. Soldiers will assume a lead role in planning BOSS events. Events should be planned that meet the needs and desires of the single soldiers.
- **Community Service**: The BOSS committee may elect to participate in community programs or projects that make a difference in the lives of others, in the community and ultimately, in themselves. The service will be voluntary in nature and in accordance with the installation volunteer program. The program can be implemented in support of existing or established volunteer programs or programs developed by the BOSS committee.
- **Quality of Life**: For single soldiers, QOL includes those actions soldiers take that directly or indirectly enhance their morale, living environment, or personal growth and development. The QOL issue identified or raised during the BOSS meetings will be directed to the appropriated command or staff agency for resolution on the installation.

AMERICAN RED CROSS

B-15. Today's American Red Cross service to the armed forces is keeping pace with the changing military through its network of 900 local chapters and 109 offices located on military installations. Both active duty and community-based military can count on the Red Cross to provide emergency

FM 7-22.7

communication services around-the-clock, 365 days a year, keeping the service member and his/her family in touch across the miles. Although we are most familiar with the Red Cross messages when there is a family emergency, the Red Cross also provides access to financial assistance through the military aid societies, counseling, information and referral and veteran's assistance. While not a part of the Department of Defense, Red Cross staff members deploy along side the military to such areas as Afghanistan, Kosovo, Saudi Arabia and Kuwait—working and living amongst the troops to ensure they receive vital Red Cross services. The Red Cross often conducts blood drives and offers a full menu of disaster and health and safety training courses. These activities are available to service members and their families at Red Cross chapters and on military installations. For additional information on Red Cross programs and services go to www.redcross.org and click on AFES (Armed Forces Emergency Services) or call toll free 1-877-272-7337.

ARMY COMMUNITY SERVICE (ACS)

B-16. Army Community Service (ACS) centers are the hub for social service programs designed to meet the needs of the America's Army family. The ACS mission is to assist commanders in maintaining readiness of individuals, families and communities within the America's Army family. They do this by developing, coordinating and delivering services. These services promote self-reliance, resiliency and stability during war and peace. ACS programs are increasingly prevention oriented, with an emphasis on working more closely with commanders. Federal law, executive order and DOD policy mandate many of the programs provided by ACS. The following ACS programs exist at Army installations worldwide—

- Mobilization and Deployment Assistance.
- Information, Referral and Follow-up Program.
- Relocation Assistance Program (RAP).
- Consumer Affairs and Financial Assistance Program (CAFAP).
- Family Member Employment Assistance Program (FMEAP).
- Exceptional Family Member Program (EFMP).
- Family Advocacy Program (FAP).
- Pre/Post Mobilization Support.
- Army Family Team Building (AFTB).
- Volunteers.
- Family Readiness Group (FRG) Program.
- Army Family Action Plan Program (AFAP).

"Knowing where to get answers is just as important as having them."

MSG Douglas E. Freed

MORALE, WELFARE AND RECREATION

B-17. The Morale, Welfare and Recreation (MWR) program improves unit readiness by promoting fitness, building morale and cohesion, enhancing quality of life and providing recreational, social and other support services for soldiers, civilians and their families. During peacetime, the scope of MWR includes sports activities, recreation centers, libraries, clubs, bowling centers, golf centers, outdoor recreation, arts and crafts and entertainment. During war and operations other than war, the MWR network provides services to the theater of operations. These services are in the form of unit recreation, library book kits, sports programs and rest areas at brigade level and higher. Military and civilian MWR personnel staff these activities and services. The MWR network also provides facilities such as unit lounges, recreation centers with snack bars and activity centers for soldiers that house a number of MWR functions.

ARMY FAMILY ACTION PLAN

B-18. The Army Family Action Plan (AFAP) is input from the people of the Army to Army leadership. It's a process that lets soldiers and families say what's working, what isn't AND what they think will fix it. It alerts commanders and Army leaders to areas of concern that need their attention, and it gives them the opportunity to quickly put plans into place to work toward resolving the issues.

- Gives commanders a gauge to validate concerns and measure satisfaction
- Enhances Army's corporate image
- Helps retain the best and brightest
- Results in legislation, policies, programs and services that strengthen readiness and retention
- Safeguards well-being

FAMILY READINESS PROGRAMS

B-19. The mission of family readiness programs is to foster total Army family readiness, as mission accomplishment is directly linked to soldiers' confidence that their families are safe and capable of carrying on during their absence. The exchange system provides basic health, hygiene and personal care needs to soldiers and Army civilians. A wide variety of resources are available to assist spouses. Access most of these through Army Knowledge Online or your unit NCO support channel:

- Married Army Couples Program.
- Unit Family Readiness Groups.
- Family Care Plans.
- Army Family Liaison Office.

- Army Family Team Building.
- Army Family Action Plan Forums.
- Family Program Academies (USAR).
- Spouse's Guide to BSB and Garrison Commands.
- Army Financial Management.
- Information and Referral programs.
- Budget counseling.
- Emergency Financial Assistance Resources.
- Counseling and Counseling Referrals.
- Child and Spouse Abuse Treatment and Prevention.
- Employment Assistance.
- Exceptional Family Member Program.
- Relocation Assistance.
- Deployment and Mobilization Support.

Appendix C

Leader Book

C-1. The leader book is a tool for the NCO to maintain up-to-date, easy-to-reference information on soldiers, training status, maintenance status and equipment accountability. There are many versions of the leader book both in official Army publications and on the commercial market. Your unit may have example forms already. In the following pages you will find example forms that may be useful in building your leader book.

C-2. Leaders are responsible for providing training assessments to the chain of command on their soldiers and units. Commanders use these assessments to make training decisions. The leader book gives leaders a tool that efficiently tracks soldier, training and equipment status.

C-3. The leader book is a tool for recording and tracking soldier proficiency on mission-oriented tasks. The exact composition of leader books varies depending on the mission and type of unit. Use the leader book to:

- Track and evaluate soldiers' training status and proficiency on essential soldier tasks.
- Provide administrative input to the chain of command on the proficiency of the unit; for example platoon, squad or crew.
- Conduct soldier performance counseling.

ORGANIZATION

C-4. The organization of the leader book is up to each individual leader. To be effective they must be well organized and "user friendly." Only essential training information should be in the leader book. Your unit may require additional items to this recommended organization:

SECTION 1: Administrative soldier data.
SECTION 2: Training Guidance, Company METL/PLT supporting collective task list with assessments.
SECTION 3: CTT proficiency (survival skills).
SECTION 4: Essential soldier task proficiency and status.
SECTION 5: Unit collective task proficiency.
SECTION 6: Equipment accountability and status.

FM 7-22.7

ADMINISTRATIVE SOLDIER DATA

C-5. Administrative soldier data sheets contain everything leaders need to know about their soldiers. The Standard Army Training System (SATS) can generate such a list or the leader can make one. Recommended information for soldier data sheets includes the following:

- Name, rank, age, TIS, TIG, DOR and duty position.
- Current weapon qualification.
- APFT score/date.
- Height/weight data.
- Family data.
- Special medical data.

COMPANY METL/PLT SUPPORTING COLLECTIVE TASK LIST

C-6. Leaders need to maintain copies of both company METL and platoon supporting collective task lists in their leader books. Having these lists and current assessments helps leaders select the appropriate individual and collective tasks that require training emphasis. This list can be in any format that the leader chooses. A recommended technique is to list the task, the current assessment and also a "why" for the assessment.

COMMON TASK TEST PROFICIENCY

C-7. Common Task Test (CTT) proficiency is critical information for all leaders. GO/NO GO data should be recorded for each soldier, along with the date of the evaluation. Knowing this information allows leaders to select appropriate opportunity training. Since company headquarters maintain individual soldiers' DA Forms 5164, leaders must develop their own system for tracking CTT proficiency.

ESSENTIAL SOLDIER TASK PROFICIENCY

C-8. Leaders select and track the proficiency of MOS-specific tasks that support the company METL/platoon supporting collective task list. By knowing the exact status of these essential tasks leaders can quickly identify weaknesses and plan and conduct training to improve proficiency.

C-9. The Standard Army Training System (SATS) provides assessment sheets that support some MTPs and ARTEP manuals. If SATS does not have an automated MTP for a particular unit, then leaders must develop their own tracking forms. The same information that is found on the SATS form should be reflected on the self-developed form.

UNIT COLLECTIVE TASK PROFICIENCY

C-10. Leaders must know the proficiency of their units to perform the collective tasks and drills that support the platoon supporting collective task list. Leaders derive section/squad/crew collective tasks from the applicable MTPs. Units without a published MTP must determine for themselves which collective tasks and drills support the platoon supporting collective tasks. In many cases the section/squad/crew collective task list will be identical to the platoon list.

C-11. SATS does not provide a collective task proficiency tracking form. Recommended information for collective task proficiency forms includes:

- Collective task.
- Assessment blocks (T-P-U or GO/NO GO).
- Date training last executed.
- Reason for assessment/strategy to improve.
- Training Assessment Model.

SOLDIER COUNSELING FORMS AND STATUS

C-12. Soldier counseling is an essential element of a leader's duties. The leader book is a natural focal point for performance counseling. Leaders strive to link counseling to demonstrated performance and the leader book provides the necessary training information. The extent that counseling can be tracked with the leader book is the leader's decision. Some leaders may want to maintain the DA Form 2166-8-1, NCO Counseling Checklist/Record, for each subordinate NCO and the DA Form 4856-E, Developmental Counseling Form, for each soldier.

C-13. Another technique is to keep a log of soldier counseling sessions in the leader book. Leaders still use the leader book to assist in counseling, but maintain the actual counseling forms in a separate file. This provides the leader an easy reference for periodic assessments and feedback and tracking new soldiers' progress.

EQUIPMENT ACCOUNTABILITY AND STATUS

C-14. This is a listing of sensitive items, vehicles and other key equipment with the soldier responsible for each and the status of each item. Don't forget to check the serial numbers on sensitive items.

LEADER BOOK APPLICATIONS

DAILY EVALUATIONS AND SOLDIER COUNSELING

C-15. Leader books are an integral part of everyday training. Leaders habitually carry their leader books with them during the training day. Shortly after training is evaluated leaders update the appropriate section of their leader book. By keeping up with the current status of the training of their soldiers, leaders can give timely and accurate assessments to their leaders.

COMPANY AND PLATOON TRAINING MEETINGS

C-16. Leader books are "part of the uniform" for both company and platoon training meetings. Accurate leader books add credibility to training assessments and form the basis for requesting training. Good leader books serve as a tool for leaders to determine what tasks need training and what tasks do not.

NOTE:
Leader books are leader business, not inspector's business. They should not be formally inspected. Their periodic review by the chain of command is appropriate. Leaders should not lose sight of the purpose of the leader book—that of being a self-designed tool to assist leaders in tracking the training proficiency of their soldiers. They come in many shapes and forms; there is no approved solution or format. To formally inspect them would be inappropriate.

_____ Leader Book

Example Leader Book Blank Pages

Daily Status Report	C-6
Personal Data Sheet	C-7
Promotion Data	C-8
Counseling Data	C-9
Common Task Test Results	C-10
Weapon Density and Training Status	C-11
Army Physical Fitness Test Data	C-12
Vehicle Status	C-13
Sensitive Item Data	C-14
8 Steps to Training	C-15
Chain of Command and NCO Support Channel	C-16
Troop Leading Procedures	C-18
Five Paragraph Operations Order	C-20
Risk Management Matrix	C-22

Example Daily Status Report

| ASSIGNED _____ SICK CALL _____ |
| ATTACHED _____ HOSPITAL _____ |
| LEAVE/PASS _____ AWOL/DESERTION _____ |
| FIELD DUTY _____ PRESENT FOR DUTY _____ |

NAME	RANK	DUTY STATUS

_____ Leader Book

Example Personal Data Sheet

NAME:_____ SSN:_____ RANK:_____ DATE ASSIGNED _____
INITIAL COUNSELING DATE: _____ 1SG/CDR INBRIEF DATE:_____
CSM/BN CDR INBRIEF DATE: _____ SECURITY CLEARANCE: _____
DATE OF LAST NCOER (ENDING MONTH): _____ NEXT NCOER DUE: _____
PULHES: _____ HT: _____ WT: _____ BLOOD TYPE: _____ DOB: _____
RELIGIOUS PREFERENCE: _____ GT: _____ PMOS: _____ SMOS: _____
ASI: _____ BPED: _____ BASD: _____ DEROS: _____ ETS: _____
DUTY POSITION: _____ PARA/LINE NUMBER _____ / _____
HISTORY OF: HEAT INJURY _____ COLD INJURY _____
LAST HIV TEST: _____ LAST DENTAL EXAM: _____ CAT: _____
CIVILIAN EDUCATION LEVEL: _____
MILITARY SCHOOLS: _____
MILITARY AWARDS: _____
CIVILIAN DRIVER'S LICENSE NUMBER: _____ STATE OF ISSUE:_____
POV TYPE AND MAKE: _____ LAST POV INSPECTION: _____
POV INSURANCE POLICY NUMBER: _____ EXPIRATION DATE: _____
MILITARY DRIVER'S LICENSE ISSUED: _____
TYPE OF VEHICLES LICENSED FOR: _____
COLD WEATHER DRIVER'S TRAINING DATE:_____
TYPE OF PERSONAL WEAPON ISSUED: _____
WEAPON SERIAL NUMBER: _____ RACK NUMBER: _____
PERSONAL WEAPON QUALIFICATION RATING: EXP / SHARP / MARKSMAN
WEAPON QUALIFICATION DATE: _____
PROTECTIVE MASK TYPE: _____ SIZE: _____ MASK NUMBER:_____
DATE MASK FITTED: _____ MOPP GEAR SIZE: TOP: _____ BOTTOM:_____
SHOES: _____ GLOVES: _____ GLASSES: YES / NO INSERTS: _____
MILITARY CLOTHING ISSUE INVENTORY DATE:_____
SHORT TERM GOALS (1-5 YEARS):_____
LONG TERM GOALS (5-10 YEARS): _____
HOBBIES: _____
MARITAL STATUS: SINGLE / MARRIED / DIVORCED/ WIDOWED ANNIV DATE: _____
SPOUSE'S NAME: _____ NUMBER OF DEPENDENTS:_____
NUMBER OF COMMAND SPONSORED DEPENDENTS: _____
CHILDREN'S NAMES AND AGES: _____

TYPE OF QUARTERS: GOVERNMENT / GOVERNMENT LEASED / LOCAL ECONOMY
HOME PHONE NUMBER: _____ WORK PHONE NUMBER:_____
EMAIL: _____ LOCAL ADDRESS:_____

NEXT OF KIN'S NAME: _____
NEXT OF KIN'S ADDRESS:_____
NEXT OF KIN'S PHONE NUMBER (INCLUDE AREA CODE): _____
NEXT OF KIN'S RELATIONSHIP: _____
HOME OF RECORD:_____

OTHER INFORMATION:_____
_____
_____

FM 7-22.7

Example Promotion Data

NAME	RANK	DOR	ELIGIBLE DATE	POINTS	REMARKS

_____ Leader Book

Example Counseling Data

NAME	RANK	DATE OF LAST COUNSELING	DATE OF NEXT COUNSELING	REMARKS

FM 7-22.7

Example Common Task Test Results

NAME	RANK	DATE	GO	NO GO	RETEST DATE

_____ Leader Book

Example Weapon Density and Training Status

NAME	M16	M9	SAW	MK 19	M60	NBC

FM 7-22.7

Example Army Physical Fitness Test Data

NAME	RANK	AGE	PU Raw/Pts	SU Raw/Pts	RUN Raw/Pts	TOT

_____ Leader Book

Example Vehicle Status

TYPE	BUMPER NUMBER	OPERATIONAL STATUS	COMMO STATUS	NEXT SERVICE DUE

FM 7-22.7 _____

Example Sensitive Items Data

ITEM	SERIAL NUMBER	LAST INV	REMARKS

_____ Leader Book

Example 8 Steps to Training

PLAN TRAINING:
TEACH THE TRAINERS:
RECON THE TRAINING SITE:
ISSUE OPORD FOR TRAINING:
REHEARSE TRAINING:
EXECUTE TRAINING:
CONDUCT AAR:
RETRAIN UNTIL STANDARD IS MET:
COMMENTS:

FM 7-22.7

The Chain of Command and NCO Support Channel

Chain of Command	*NCO Support Channel*
Commander in Chief: _____	
Secretary of Defense: _____	
Chairman, Joint Chiefs: _____	
Secretary of the Army: _____	
Army Chief of Staff: _____	SMA: _____
Theater/MACOM CDR: _____	CSM: _____
Corps CDR: _____	CSM: _____
DIV CDR: _____	CSM: _____
BDE CDR: _____	CSM: _____
BN CDR: _____	CSM: _____
Co/Bty/Trp CDR: _____	1SG: _____
PLT LDR: _____	PSG: _____

Squad / Section / Team Leader: _____

_____ **Leader Book**

FM 7-22.7

Troop Leading Procedures

STEP 1. **Receive the Mission**. This may be in the form of a Warning Order (WARNORD), an Operation Order (OPORD), or a Fragmentary Order (FRAGO). Analyze it using the factors of Mission, Enemy, Terrain, Troops, Time available and Civilian considerations (METT-TC).
    (1) Use no more than one third of the available time for planning and issuing the operation order.
    (2) Determine what are the specified tasks (you were told to accomplish), the essential tasks (must accomplish to succeed) and the implied tasks (necessary but not spelled out).
    (3) Plan preparation activity backward from the time of execution.

STEP 2. **Issue a Warning Order**. Provide initial instructions to your soldiers in a WARNORD. Include all available information and update as often as necessary. Certain information must be in the warning order:
    (1) The mission or nature of the operation.
    (2) Participants in the operation.
    (3) Time of the operation.
    (4) Time and place for issuance of the operation order.

STEP 3. **Make a Tentative Plan**. Gather and consider key information for use in making a tentative plan. Update the information continuously and refine the plan as needed. Use this plan as the starting point for coordination, reconnaissance and movement instructions. Consider the factors of METT-TC:
    (1) *Mission*. Review the mission to ensure you fully understand all tasks.
    (2) *Enemy*. Consider the type, size, organization, tactics and equipment of the enemy. Identify the greatest threat to the mission and their greatest vulnerability.
    (3) *Terrain*. Consider the effects of terrain and weather using Observation, Concealment, Obstacles, Key Terrain and Avenues of Approach (OCOKA).
    (4) *Troops available*. Consider the strength of subordinate units, the characteristics of weapon systems and the capabilities of attached elements when assigning tasks to subordinate units.
    (5) *Time available*. Refine the allocation of time based on the tentative plan and any changes to the situation.
    (6) *Civilian considerations*. Consider the impact of the local population or other civilians on operations.

STEP 4. **Start Necessary Movement**. Get the unit moving to where it needs to be as soon as possible.

STEP 5. **Reconnoiter**. If time allows, make a personal reconnaissance to verify your terrain analysis, adjust the plan, confirm the usability of routes and time any critical movements. Otherwise, make a map reconnaissance.

STEP 6. **Complete the Plan**. Complete the plan based on the reconnaissance and any changes in the situation. Review the plan to ensure it meets the commander's intent and requirements of the mission.

STEP 7. **Issue the Complete Order.** Platoon and smaller unit leaders normally issue oral operations orders. See page 162 for the Operations Order format.

(1) To aid soldiers in understanding the concept for the mission, try to issue the order within sight of the objective or on the defensive terrain. When this is not possible, use a terrain model or sketch.

(2) Ensure that your soldiers understand the mission, the commander's intent, the concept of the operation and their assigned tasks. You might require soldiers to repeat all or part of the order or demonstrate on the model or sketch their understanding of the operation.

STEP 8. **Supervise.** Supervise preparation for combat by conducting rehearsals and inspections.

(1) *Rehearsals.* Use rehearsals to practice essential tasks, reveal weaknesses or problems in the plan and improve soldier understanding of the concept of the operation.

- Rehearsals should include subordinate leaders briefing their planned actions in sequence.
- Conduct rehearsals on terrain that resembles the actual ground and in similar light conditions.

(2) *Inspections.* Conduct pre-combat checks and inspections. Inspect—

- Weapons, ammunition, uniforms and equipment.
- Mission-essential equipment.
- Soldier's understanding of the mission and their specific responsibilities.
- Communications.
- Rations and water.
- Camouflage.
- Deficiencies noted during earlier inspections.

FM 7-22.7 _____

The Five Paragraph Operations Order (OPORD)

An OPORD gives the subordinate leaders the essential information needed to carry out an operation. OPORDs use a five-paragraph format to organize thoughts and ensure completeness. They also help subordinate leaders understand and follow the order. Use a terrain model or sketch along with a map to explain the order.

TASK ORGANIZATION:
(The company or battalion task organization for the mission is stated at the start of the OPORD so that the subordinates know what assets they will have during the operation.)

1. SITUATION.
a. **Enemy Situation.**
    (1) Composition, disposition, and strength.
    (2) Recent activities.
    (3) Capabilities.
    (4) The enemy's most probable COA. A sketch or enemy overlay is normally included to clarify this description.
b. **Friendly Situation.**
    (1) Mission and concept for the battalion.
    (2) Mission for the unit on the left.
    (3) Mission for the unit on the right.
    (4) Mission for the unit to the front.
    (5) Mission for the unit to the rear or following.
    (6) Mission for the battalion reserve.
    (7) Mission for any units supporting the battalion if they impact on the mission.
c. **Attachments and Detachments.** Changes to the task organization during the operation. For example, if the task organization changes during the consolidation phase of an attack, it would be indicated here.

2. MISSION.
The mission essential task(s) and purpose(s). It normally includes Who, What, When, Where, and Why. The where is described in terms of terrain features/grid coordinates. If objective names are used, they are secondary references and placed in parentheses.

3. EXECUTION.
a. **Concept of the Operation.** This paragraph describes how the leader intends to accomplish his mission. At company level, a maneuver and fires subparagraph will always be included. The operation overlay/concept sketch is referenced here.
    (1) *Maneuver.* The maneuver paragraph should be focused on the decisive action. At company level, a maneuver paragraph that outlines the missions to each platoon and or section and identifies the main effort normally, requires no additional clarification. If it should, the leader may clarify it in the concept of the operation paragraph (paragraph 3a).
    (2) *Fires.* This paragraph describes how the leader intends for the fires to support the maneuver. It normally states the purpose to be achieved by the fires, the

priority of fires, and the allocation of any priority targets. A target list, fires execution matrix, or target overlay may be referenced here.

(3) ***Engineering.*** Often, especially in defensive operations, this paragraph is required to clarify the concept for preparing fortifications. When engineers support the mortar platoon or section, the leader states his guidance for employing these assets here. He may do this by stating his priority for the engineer effort (survivability, countermobility, and mobility) and the priority for supporting the sections.

b. **Tasks to Sections or Squads.** This paragraph lists each of the section's tasks/limitations. Each subordinate unit will have a separate paragraph.

c. **Coordinating Instructions.** These are the tasks and limitations that apply to two or more subordinate units. If they do not apply to all the subordinate units, then those units that must comply are clearly stated.

4. SERVICE SUPPORT.

This paragraph provides the critical logistical information required to sustain the unit during the operation.

a. **General.** It provides current and future trains locations.

b. **Materiel and Services.** It may have a separate subparagraph for each class of supply, as required.

c. **Casualty Evacuation.**

d. **Miscellaneous.**

5. COMMAND AND SIGNAL.

a. **Command.** This paragraph states where the C2 facilities and key personnel will be located during the operation and adjustments to the unit SOP, such as a change to the succession of command or the standard wire plan.

b. **Signal.** It provides critical communication requirements such as radio listening silence in effect forward of the LD, signals for specific events or actions, emergency/visual signals for critical actions, and SOI information.

ACKNOWLEDGE. Use the message reference number.

ANNEXES
A-Intelligence/Intelligence Overlay(s).
B-Operation Overlay/Concept Sketches.
C-As required, such as road march, truck/boat movement, air assault, and river crossing.

FM 7-22.7

Risk Management Matrix

Risk E - Extremely High H - High M - Moderate L - Low		HAZARD PROBABILITY				
		Frequent	Likely	Occasional	Seldom	Unlikely
S E V E R I T Y	Catastrophic	E	E	H	H	M
	Critical	E	H	H	M	L
	Marginal	H	M	M	L	L
	Negligible	M	L	L	L	L

HAZARD PROBABILITY (The likelihood that an event will occur).

Frequent -- The event occurs often in a soldier's career or is continuously experienced by all soldiers exposed.

Likely – There is a good possibility that an event will occur several times in a soldier's career and is experienced a lot by the soldiers exposed.

Occasional -- The event occurs once in a while such as, once in the career of a soldier, or sporadically to all soldiers exposed.

Seldom – There is a remote possibility that an event will occur in the career of a soldier. For a fleet or inventory, it would be unlikely but can be expected and would occur seldom to all soldiers exposed.

Unlikely -- The possibility that an event would occur to in the career of a soldier is so rare that you can assume that it will not occur. It would most likely not occur within the fleet or inventory and very rarely occurs to all soldiers exposed.

SEVERITY (The expected consequence of an event in terms of degree of injury, property damage or other mission-impairing factors).

Catastrophic -- results in death or permanent total disability, a systems loss, or major property damage.

Critical – results in severe injury. That is, permanent partial disability or temporary total disability in excess of three months for personnel, and major systems damage or significant property damage.

Marginal -- results in minor injury or lost workday accident for personnel. Minor systems or property damage.

Negligible -- first aid or less required. Minor systems impairment.

RISK LEVELS

E (Extremely High) – Loss of ability to accomplish mission.
H (High) – Significant degradation of mission capabilities in terms of required mission standard.
M (Moderate) – Degradation of mission capabilities in terms of required mission standards.
L (Low) – Little or no impact on accomplishment of mission.

Appendix D

Internet Resources

D-1. The Internet is a remarkable conduit to a vast storehouse of knowledge. Through the Internet an NCO can find out how to conduct a developmental counseling session, where the housing office is at his next assignment or communicate with a Motor Sergeant in the Republic of Korea who developed a better way of issuing replacement parts.

D-2. These websites are in the categories of General, Leadership, Assistance, Personnel, Training, History, News and Unit sites. Site addresses on the Internet often change without warning, but you can link to most of these sites through the Army Homepage, Army Knowledge Online or the Sergeants Major Academy Homepage.

GENERAL

Army Knowledge Online – http://www.us.army.mil
  * *Get your Army-wide email account here.*
Army Homepage – http://www.army.mil
  * *The Army Homepage links to nearly every other official Army site.*
Army National Guard Homepage – http://www.arng.army.mil/
Army Reserve Homepage – http://www.army.mil/usar
Reimer Digital Library — http://www.adtdl.army mil/atdls.htm
  * *The Digital Library has electronic versions of most FMs, TCs and other training documents for online viewing or download.*
US Army Publishing Agency – http://www.usapa.army mil
  * *Find ARs, DAPAMs and other Army administrative publications.*
Army Values – http://www.dtic.mil/armylink/graphics/values.html
Army Vision – http://www.army mil/vision/default htm
Army Transformation – http://www.lewis.army.mil/transformation/index.html
Worldwide Locator – http://www.erec.army mil/wwl/default htm
  * *Find active and reserve soldiers around the world.*

LEADERSHIP

US Army Sergeants Major Academy – http://usasma.bliss.army.mil
  * *Find information on NCO matters, The NCO Journal Online and information on NCO Academies.*
The Army Leadership Homepage – http://www.leadership.army mil
The Army Counseling Homepage – http://www.counseling.army.mil
Center for Army Leadership – http://www-cgsc.army mil/cal/index.htm

ASSISTANCE

Army Career and Alumni Program – http://www.acap.army.mil/

Army Emergency Relief – http://www.aerhq.org
Education – http://www.armyeducation.army.mil/
Delta Dental – http://www.deltadental.com/
GI Bill – http://www.gibill.va.gov
Mobilization – http://www.defenselink mil/ra/mobil/
Morale, Welfare and Recreation – http://www.armymwr.com/
Tricare – http://www.tricare.osd mil/

PERSONNEL

Assignments – https://www.perscomonline.army.mil/
Career Management – https://www.perscomonline.army.mil/enlist/enlist htm
Department of Veterans Affairs – http://www.va.gov/
Military Records – https://etransserv.erec.army mil/
NCOER – https://www.perscomonline.army.mil/select/ncoer.htm
Pay Chart – http://www.dfas.mil/money/milpay/pay/bp-1.htm
Pay Issues – https://emss.dfas mil/emss htm
Promotions – https://www.perscomonline.army mil/select/enlisted htm
Retirement Services –
http://www.odcsper.army.mil/Directorates/retire/retire1.asp

TRAINING

NCO Academies – https://www.perscom.army.mil/epncoes/ncoalink htm
Battle Command Training Program – http://bctp.leavenworth.army.mil/
Combat Maneuver Training Center – http://www.cmtc.7atc.army mil/
Joint Readiness Training Center – http://www.jrtc-polk.army.mil/
National Training Center – http://www.irwin.army mil/
Center for Army Lessons Learned – http://call.army.mil

HISTORY

Army Center for Military History – http://www.army mil/cmh-pg
Military History Institute – http://carlisle-www.army.mil/usamhi/
NCO Museum – http://usasma.bliss.army.mil/museum/

NEWS

Army News – http://www.dtic.mil/armylink
Army Newswatch – http://www.army mil/newswatch.htm
Soldiers Radio and TV – http://www.army.mil/videos/
Defense News – http://www.defenselink.mil
Early Bird News – http://ebird.dtic.mil
NCO Journal – http://usasma.bliss.army.mil/Journal/

UNIT SITES

US Army Training and Doctrine Command – http://www.tradoc.army.mil/
US Army Forces Command – http://www.forscom.army.mil/
US Army Pacific Command – http://www.usarpac.army.mil/
US Army Southern Command – http://www.usarso.army.mil/
US Army, Europe – http://www.hqusareur.army.mil/
Eighth US Army – http://www.korea.army.mil/eusa/default.htm
US Army Forces Central Command – http://www.arcent.army.mil/
US Army Medical Command (MEDCOM) – http://www.armymedicine.army.mil/armymed
US Army Corps of Engineers – http://www.usace.army.mil/
Military Traffic Management Command – http://www.mtmc.army.mil/
I Corps – http://www.lewis.army.mil/
III Corps – http://pao.hood.army.mil/
V Corps – http://www.hq.c5.army.mil/
XVIII Airborne Corps – http://www.bragg.army.mil/18abn/default.htm

Appendix E

NCO Reading List

E-1. Every leader in the Army can become better at leading soldiers. Reading books and articles by and about combat leaders can give good insight into improving leadership skills. One should be familiar, too, with the documents that our Nation was founded on – the Constitution and the Declaration of Independence. Reading about past leaders and knowing our history as a Nation and Army lets you better understand your role as an NCO. It also lets you realize that many soldiers before you encountered and overcame some of the same problems you face.

RECOMMENDED PROFESSIONAL DEVELOPMENT READING LIST FOR NCOS

E-2. This list is based on the Chief of Staff of the Army's list and that of the Sergeant Major of the Army. The list may change from time to time. For an up-to-date list, see the Sergeants Major Academy Homepage at http:\\usasma.bliss.army.mil.

CPL - SGT

Stephen E. Ambrose, *Band of Brothers: E Company, 506th Regiment, 101st Airborne from Normandy to Hitler's Eagle's Nest.* New York: Simon & Schuster, 1992. (335 pages)

Tom Brokaw, *The Greatest Generation.* New York: Random House, 1998. (412 pages)

T. R. Fehrenbach, *This Kind of War: A Study in Unpreparedness.* Washington, DC: Brassey's Inc. 1994 (483 pages)

Charles E. Heller and William A. Stoft, editors, *America's First Battles: 1776-1965.* Lawrence, KS: University Press of Kansas. 1986. (416 pages)

David W. Hogan, Jr., *225 Years of Service, The US Army 1775-2000.* Washington, DC: Center for Military History, 2000. (36 pages)

John Keegan, *The Face of Battle.* New York: Vintage Books, 1977. (354 pages)

Harold G. Moore and Joseph L. Galloway, *We Were Soldiers Once and Young.* New York: Random House. 1992. (412 pages)

Anton Myrer, *Once an Eagle*. New York: USAWC Foundation Press, 1995. (817 pages)

Michael Shaara, *The Killer Angels*. New York: Ballantine Books, 1974. (355 pages)

SSG -SFC

Stephen E. Ambrose, *Citizen Soldiers*. New York: Simon & Schuster, 1997. (480 pages)

Edward M. Coffman, *The War To End All Wars: The American Military Experience in World War I*. New York: Oxford University Press, 1968. (412 pages)

Samuel P. Huntington, *Soldier and the State*. Cambridge, MA: Belknap Press of Harvard University press, 1957. (534 pages)

Gerald F. Linderman, *Embattled Courage: The Experience of Combat in the American Civil War*. New York: The Free Press, A Division of Macmillan, 1987. (357 pages)

Charles B. MacDonald, *Company Commander*. Springfield, NJ: Burford Books, 1999. (278 pages)

S.L.A. Marshall, *Men Against Fire: The Problem of Battle Command in Future War*. Norman, OK: University of Oklahoma Press, 2000. (224 pages)

Alan R. Millett and Peter Maslowski, *For the Common Defense, A Military History of the United States of America*. New York: The Free Press, 1984. (621 pages)

Robert H. Scales, Jr., *Certain Victory*. Washington, DC: Brassey's Inc., 1998. (448 pages)

Mark A. Stoler, *George C. Marshall: Soldier-Statesman of the American Century*. Boston, MA: Twayne Publishers, 1989. (252 pages)

Tom Willard, *Buffalo Soldiers*. New York: Forge Press, 1997. (336 pages)

MSG - CSM

Roy E. Appleman, *East of Chosin: Entrapment and Breakout in Korea, 1950.* College Station, TX: Texas A&M University Press, 1987. (399 pages)

Graham A. Cosmas, *An Army for Empire: The United States Army and the Spanish American War.* Shippensburg, PA: White Mane, 1994. (349 pages)

Robert A. Doughty, *The Evolution of US Army Tactical Doctrine, 1946-1976.* Fort Leavenworth, Kansas: Combat Studies Institute, 1979. (57 pages)

Antoine Henri Jomini, *Jomini and His Summary of the Art of War.* Harrisburg, Pennsylvania: Stackpole Books, 1965. (161 pages)

Charles B. MacDonald and Sidney T. Mathews, *Three Battles: Arnaville, Altuzzo and Schmidt.* Washington, DC: Center of Military History, 1952. (443 pages)

James M. McPherson, *Battle Cry of Freedom: The Civil War Era.* New York: Oxford University Press, 1988. (904 pages):

Roger H. Nye, *The Challenge of Command.* Wayne, New Jersey: Avery Publishing Group, 1986. (187 pages)

Dave R. Palmer, *Summons of the Trumpet: US-Vietnam in Perspective.* San Rafael, CA: Presidio Press, 1978. (277 pages)

Martin Van Creveld, *Supplying War: Logistics from Wallenstein to Patton.* New York: Cambridge University Press, 1977. (284 pages)

Russell F. Weigley, *The American Way of War: A History of United States Military Strategy and Policy.* Bloomington: Indiana University Press, 1977. (477 pages)

OTHER BOOKS OF INTEREST TO THE NCO

William G. Bainbridge, *Top Sergeant: The Life and Times of Sergeant Major of the Army William G. Bainbridge.* New York: Ballantine Books, 1995. (357 pages)

Roy Benavidez, *The Three Wars of Roy Benavidez.* San Antonio, TX: Corona Publishing Company, 1986. (293 pages)

Stephen Crane, *The Red Badge of Courage: An Episode of the American Civil War*. New York: Random House, 1998 (reissue). (308 pages)

Arnold G. Fisch, Jr., *The Story of the Noncommissioned Officer Corps: The Backbone of the Army*. Washington, DC: Center of Military History, 1989. (250 pages)

Ernest F. Fisher, Jr., *Guardians of the Republic: A History of the Noncommissioned Officer Corps of the US Army*. Mechanicsburg, PA: Stackpole Books, 2001 (475 pages)

Mark F. Gillespie et al, *The Sergeants Major of the Army*. Washington, DC: Center of Military History, 1995. (180 pages) (new edition due in 2003)

Sun Tzu and Sun Pin, *The Complete Art of War*. Boulder, CO: Westview Press, 1996. (304 pages)

Appendix F

NCO Induction Ceremony

F-1. The NCO induction ceremony is a celebration of the newly promoted joining the ranks of a professional noncommissioned officer corps and emphasizes and builds on the pride we all share as members of such an elite corps. The ceremony should also serve to honor the memory of those men and women of the NCO Corps who have served with pride and distinction.

> *"A pat on the back applied at the proper moment in the circumstances can have a dramatic influence in developing leader."*
>
> SMA William G. Bainbridge

F-2. Induction ceremonies should in no way be used as an opportunity for hazing, but more as a rite of passage. It allows fellow NCOs of a unit to build and develop a cohesive bond, support team development and serve as a legacy for future NCO Induction Ceremonies.

F-3. The importance of recognizing the transition from "just one of the guys or gals" to a noncommissioned officer should be shared among the superiors, peers and soldiers of the newly promoted. The induction ceremony should be held separate and to serve as an extension of the promotion ceremony. Typical Army promotion effective dates occur on the first day of a month and when possible, so should the induction ceremony.

SETTING UP

F-4. The NCO induction ceremony is typically conducted at the Battalion (or equivalent) level. Though it can be held at higher or lower levels, this document will provide an example for a Battalion NCO induction ceremony. By changing the titles of key NCO leaders to meet your own need, you can tailor this document to your own organization.

LOCATION

F-5. Though the location of the ceremony is not as important as the content, consider the following: As part of the socialization process of newly promoted noncommissioned officers, the induction ceremony should be held in a social meeting area, such as NCO, community, or all-ranks club. Alternately, a well equipped gymnasium, post theater, or for smaller ceremonies, a unit dayroom could be used. Chapel use is discouraged to avoid perceptions of "ritualistic" or "mystic" overtones that go directly against the intended result.

FM 7-22.7

TIMING

F-6. As part of the socialization process for new noncommissioned officers, the induction ceremony should be scheduled as a training event on the training calendar. The formal portion should take place during the duty day, prior to retreat. By making it a training event during duty hours, you not only get maximum participation, but command support (Commanders approve training schedules). The optimum time is 1630 to 1700 for the formal portion (the ceremony) and 1700-1730 for the informal portion (greetings, congratulations and socializing).

KEY PERSONNEL

F-7. As the senior NCO of the command, the battalion command sergeant major serves as the host of the NCO induction ceremony. The first sergeants are the CSM's assistants and they compose the "Official Party." If desired, a guest speaker for the ceremony may be included and also is a part of the official party. A narrator will serve as the Master of Ceremonies.

INVITED GUESTS AND VIPS

F-8. As a wholly noncommissioned officer sponsored event, guests and VIPs should be limited to current and former US Army NCOs. Certain situations may warrant an officer or civilian to attend and will not detract from the nature of the occasion. Typical invited guests could include higher echelon command sergeants major (brigade, division, regimental, commandant), installation or base support battalion (BSB) command sergeants major, or even lateral (battalion level) command sergeants major. Additionally, special guests serving as motivational speakers should be included (though not required) as part of an induction ceremony.

EQUIPMENT REQUIRED

F-9. Though each ceremony can be as different as the people it recognizes can, a commonality should be shared between them. The following items should be available for each:

- A passage of a citation for bravery or valor in the face of difficulty demonstrated by a noncommissioned officer.
- Copies of the NCO Creed, one per inductee.
- FM 7-22.7, *The Army Noncommissioned Officer Guide*, one per inductee.
- Sound system, if needed. Requirement based only on the number present and the "command voice" of the participants.
- Programs (including the words to the NCO Creed) if desired.

CEREMONY CONDUCT

F-10. Appendix F and the example ceremony it contains provide a common basis from which to begin. Tailor it to suit your specific needs. The goal is to present a professional and memorable NCO induction ceremony.

- **PLACES:** Official party – Waiting outside the ceremony room.

    Narrator – At the sound system/podium.

    Inductees – Formed in advance at an appropriate location. Each should have a copy (or portion) of the NCO Creed.

    (2-minutes before ceremony begins)

- **NARRATOR:** Ladies and Gentlemen, the ceremony will begin in two minutes. (At the predetermined time)

- **NARRATOR:** Please rise for the official party.

    (Official party arrives, marches to designated location. Stops, then takes appropriate positions)

- **NARRATOR:** Welcome to (this months) (month name) NCO induction ceremony where we recognize the passing of the group before you (the inductees) into the ranks of the time-honored United States Army Noncommissioned Officer Corps. Today's official party consists of (names). The tradition of commemorating the passing of a soldier to a noncommissioned officer can be traced to the Army of Frederick the Great. Before one could be recognized in the full status of an NCO, he was required to stand four watches, one every four days.

    At the first watch the private soldiers appeared and claimed a gift of bread and brandy. The company NCOs came to the second watch for beer and tobacco and the First Sergeant reserved his visit for the third watch, when he was presented with a glass of wine and a piece of tobacco on a tin plate1. Today, we commemorate this rite of passage as a celebration of the newly promoted joining the ranks of a professional noncommissioned officer corps and emphasize and build on the pride we all share as members of such an elite corps. We also serve to honor the memory of those men and women of the NCO Corps who have served with pride and distinction. Today, we remember one of our own, one whose courage should not go unremembered:

- **NARRATOR:** (read citation. Include name, unit, etc.)

- **NARRATOR:** Since the earliest days of our Army, the noncommissioned officer has been recognized as one who instills discipline and order within a unit. Baron Friedrich von Steuben, the US Army's first "Drill-Master" listed in his *Regulations for the Order and Discipline of the Troops of the United States*, the **Blue Book** that: "Each Sergeant and Corporal will be answerable for the squad committed to his care. He must pay particular attention to their conduct in every respect and that they keep themselves and their arms always clean. In dealing with recruits, they must exercise all their patience and while on the march, the noncommissioned officers must preserve order and regularity."

FM 7-22.7

Today, we continue that tradition. (Name), our (guest speaker)(CSM) now will share his/her instructions with our newest sergeants and corporals.

- **SPEAKER:** (motivational speech)
- **NARRATOR:** The Creed of the Noncommissioned Officer has served as a guiding document for noncommissioned officers since its inception in 1973, though its concepts have been always been a part of our Corps. Each major paragraph begins with three letters: N, C and O. These words have inspired noncommissioned officers and have served as a compass to guide us down the right paths that we encounter. Today, our newest noncommissioned officers will affirm their commitment to the professionalism of our corps and become a part of the "Backbone" of the Army.

    (Inductees rise)

    (Have all present read the NCO Creed together.) Note: provide copies in advance to all present.

- **CSM/HOST:** Moves to each inductee, issues them a copy of FM 7-22.7, *The Army Noncommissioned Officer Guide*, then shakes their hand and congratulates them.
- **ALL PRESENT:** Applause.
- **NARRATOR:** As we conclude today's ceremony, we ask you to greet our newest inductees and join us in welcoming them to the Corps. Please rise for the exit of the official party.
- **OFFICIAL PARTY:** (Departs. Ceremony ends. Informal portion begins -- socializing).

"Some of the old soldiers out there who have perhaps grown a bit cynical and too sophisticated for ceremonies think you have the option to decline a ceremony for yourself.

'Sir, just give the orders and I'll sew on my stripes tonight in the privacy of my home,' you might say; or 'Sir, don't go to the trouble of setting up an ceremony: you can just give me the stripe right here in your office.'

Does that sound familiar? Stop a minute to consider how selfless you are supposed to be as a leader. A military ceremony is not yours even if you are the sole reason for the ceremony. It belongs to all the soldiers. Don't miss any opportunity to stop and recognize well-deserving soldiers, especially the opportunity to reward young soldiers receiving their first awards or advancements a simple tradition of our Army packed with a powerful stimulus for soldiers."

CSM Joshua Perry

The History of the NCO Creed

The Creed has existed in different versions for a number of years. Long into their careers, sergeants remember reciting the NCO Creed during their induction into the NCO Corps. Nearly every NCO's office or home has a copy hanging on a wall. Some have intricate etchings in metal on a wooden plaque, or printed in fine calligraphy. But a quick glance at any copy of the NCO Creed and you will see no author's name at the bottom. The origin of the NCO Creed is a story of its own.

In 1973, the Army (and the noncommissioned officer corps) was in turmoil. Of the post-Vietnam developments in American military policy, the most influential in shaping the Army was the advent of the Modern Volunteer Army. With the inception of the Noncommissioned Officer Candidate Course, many young sergeants were not the skilled trainers of the past and were only trained to perform a specific job; squad leaders in Vietnam. The noncommissioned officer system was under development and the army was rewriting its Field Manual 22-100, *Leadership*, to set a road map for leaders to follow.

Of those working on the challenges at hand, one of the only NCO-pure instructional departments at the U.S Army Infantry School (USAIS) at Fort Benning, Georgia, GA was the NCO Subcommittee of the Command and Leadership Committee in the Leadership Department. Besides training soldiers at the Noncommissioned Officers Academy, these NCOs also developed instructional material and worked as part of the team developing model leadership programs of instruction.

During one brainstorming session, SFC Earle Brigham recalls writing three letters on a plain white sheet of paper... N-C-O. From those three letters they began to build the NCO Creed. The idea behind developing a creed was to give noncommissioned officers a "yardstick by which to measure themselves."

When it was ultimately approved, the NCO Creed was printed on the inside cover of the special texts issued to students attending the NCO courses at Fort Benning, beginning in 1974. Though the NCO Creed was submitted higher for approval and distribution Army-wide, it was not formalized by an official army publication until 11 years later.

Though it has been rewritten in different ways, the NCO Creed still begins its paragraphs with those three letters: N-C-O. It continues to guide and reinforce the values of each new generation of noncommissioned officers.

FM 7-22.7

Source Notes

These are the sources quoted or paraphrased in this publication, listed by page number. Where Material appears in a paragraph, both page and paragraph number are shown. Boldface indicates vignette titles.

Cover photo of Revolutionary War sergeant of the 3rd New Jersey Regiment courtesy of Roger W. Smith and Delores A. Smith of the 3rd New Jersey Regiment (re-enactment group affiliated with the Brigade of the American Revolution).

Cover image of Sergeant of Riflemen rank insignia. For more information on early NCO rank insignia, see William K. Emerson (LTC, US Army), *Chevrons, Catalog of U.S. Army Insignia*, Smithsonian Institution Press, Washington DC, 1983.

vii	**Charge to the Noncommissioned Officer.** Excerpted from the Department of the Army Certificate of Promotion, DA Form 4872, Jan 2000.
xi	**Medal of Honor Citation.** Excerpted from the Medal of Honor Citation for CSM (then SFC) Gary L. Littrell. The South Vietnamese 23rd Ranger Battalion (the unit CSM Littrell was supporting at the time of the action) was in contact with elements of three North Vietnamese regiments – over 5000 enemy soldiers against 430.

Historical Vignettes

xii	**Sergeant Patrick Gass Vignette** -- L.R. Arms, Curator, US Army NCO Museum, "Sergeant Patrick Gass," May 2002.
xiii	**SGT James Rissler Vignette** -- SGT James R. Rissler, Interview, 19 June 2002.

Chapter 1 – History and Background

1-3	The section, "The History of the American NCO," is largely from L.R. Arms, Curator, US Army NCO Museum, "A Short History of the US Army Noncommissioned Officer," 1999.
1-4	Quotation of CSM Cynthia Pritchett, interview, 19 Sep 02.
1-5	**Sergeant Brown at Redoubt Number 10**, Arnold G. Fisch, Jr. and Robert K. Wright, Jr., *The Story of the Noncommissioned Officer Corps, The Backbone of the Army*. (Washington, DC: Center of Military History, 1989) (hereafter cited as *The Story of the NCO Corps*), 216.
1-7	**Sergeant William McKinley at Antietam**, *Story of the NCO Corps*, 217.
1-8	**The 54th Massachusetts Assault on Fort Wagner**, Kim A. O'Connell, "The 54th Massachusetts and the Assault on Fort Wagner." The Menare Foundation, http://www.ugrr.org/civil/cw-ess5.htm.
1-9	**Buffalo Soldiers and Sergeant George Jordan**, excerpted from the Medal of Honor Citation for Sergeant George Jordan.
1-9	**Corporal Titus in the Boxer Rebellion**, *Story of the NCO Corps*, 218.

1-11	**Sergeant Patrick Walsh in World War I**, *Story of the NCO Corps*, 219.
1-12	**Staff Sergeant Kazuo Otani at Pieve Di St. Luce**, excerpted from the Medal of Honor Citation for Staff Sergeant Kazuo Otani.
1-13	**Staff Sergeant John Sjogren at San Jose Hacienda**, excerpted from the Medal of Honor Citation for Staff Sergeant John C. Sjogren.
1-14	**Sergeant Ola Mize at 'Outpost Harry'**, excerpted from the Medal of Honor Citation for Sergeant Ola L. Mize.
1-15	**SFC Eugene Ashley at Lang Vei**, excerpted from the Medal of Honor Citation for SFC Eugene Ashley, Jr.
1-16	Story of SMA Wooldridge, in CSM Dan Elder, "Office of the Sergeant Major of the Army," *NCO Journal Online*, Fall, 2001.
1-18	**MSG Gordon and SFC Shughart at Mogadishu**, excerpted from Medal of Honor Citations for MSG Gary I. Gordon and SFC Randall D. Shughart.
1-20	**SGT Christine Roberts in Kosovo**, from LTG James B. Peake, "Army Medics Ready for Conflict." *US Medicine*, January 2002, 39.
1-21	"Large units are likely…" FM 3-0, *Operations*, June 2001 (hereafter cited as FM 3-0), 1-17.
1-22	Quotation of SMA Jack L. Tilley, Twelfth Sergeant Major of the Army, in SSG Donald Sparks, "Interview: A Talk With Sergeant Major of the Army Jack Tilley," *NCO Journal*, Winter 2001, 15.
1-22	Quotation of GEN John N. Abrams in SPC Michael Scott, "Force Protection Key to Army XXI Plan," Army News Service, June 23, 1998.
1-23	Quotation from S.L.A. Marshall, *Men Against Fire: The Problem of Battle Command in Future War*, (Gloucester, Massachusetts: Peter Smith, 1978), 200.
1-23	Quotation from GEN John A. Wickham, Jr., *Collected Works of the Thirtieth Chief of Staff of the United States Army*, (Washington, DC: US Army Center for Military History, 1996), 23.
1-23	Quotation of GEN Bruce Clarke, DA PAM 600-65, "Leadership Statements and Quotes," 1985, 5.
1-24	Quotation of GA Omar N. Bradley, in *Military Review*, May 1948, 62.
1-24	Quotation of LTG Thomas J. Jackson, in Robert Debs Heinl, *Dictionary of Military and Naval Quotations* (Annapolis, MD: US Naval Institute Press, 1988), 151.
1-24	Quotation from GEN J. Lawton Collins, *Lightning Joe: An Autobiography*, (Baton Rouge, LA: Louisiana State University Press, 1979), 444.
1-25	Quotation from SMA William Connelly, Sixth Sergeant Major of the Army, "NCOs: Its Time to Get Tough," *ARMY Magazine* (October 1981), 31.
1-25	1-58. "…compels the soldier to fight through…" Proposed definition of the warrior ethos, "The Army Training and Leader Development Panel (NCO), Final Report," 2 April 2002, para 76 (hereafter cited as ATLDP NCO Report).
1-25	**Corporal Rodolfo Hernandez on Hill 420**, excerpt from the Medal of Honor Citation for CPL Rodolfo P. Hernandez.
1-26	"Noncommissioned officers, properly…" Report of the Secretary of War, 1888, 142.
1-26	Figure 1-1. Structured Self-development Program Briefing, 14 Dec 01.

Source Notes

1-27 Quotation of Col. Kenneth Simpson and CSM Oren Bevins, Commandant and CSM, USASMA, Oct 1989.

1-28 Quotation of MSG Henry Caro, Excellence in Leadership Awardee, SMC Class No. 2, 1974.

1-29 "You must learn more..." *The Noncom's Guide,* (Harrisburg, PA: Stackpole Books, 1948), 16. This was the predecessor to *The NCO Guide, 7th Edition,* by the same publisher.

1-29 CSM George D. Mock and SFC John K. D'Amato, "Building the Force: 'Skill, Will and Teamwork.'" *NCO Journal,* Summer 1991, 18.

Chapter 2 – Duties, Responsibilities and Authority of the NCO

2-3 2-4. TC 22-6, *The Army Noncommissioned Officer Guide,* November 1990 (hereafter cited as TC 22-6), 5.

2-4 2-6. FM 22-600-20, *The Army Noncommissioned Officer Guide,* March 1980 (hereafter cited as FM 22-600-20, 1980), 24.

2-4 Quotation from Drill Sergeant Karl Baccene, "It's Tough to Be the First Domino," *ARMY,* FEB 1971, 41.

2-5 Quotation from SMA Leon L. Van Autreve, Fourth Sergeant Major of the Army, in "The Army's SMAs from the Beginning to the Present." *NCO Journal,* Summer 1994, pp. 10-11.

2-5 2-9. FM 6-22 (FM 22-100), *Leadership,* August 1999 (hereafter cited as FM 6-22), 2-23.

2-5 2-11, 2-12. DA Pamphlet 600-25, "NCO Development Program," April 1987 (hereafter cited as DA PAM 600-25, 1987), 12.

2-6 "Rank is a badge..." DA Pam 360-1, "Know Your Army," 1957 (hereafter cited as DA PAM 360-1, 1957), 6.

2-7 Quotation from SMA Richard A. Kidd, Ninth Sergeant Major of the Army, in "The Army's SMAs from the Beginning to the Present," *NCO Journal,* Summer 1994, 13.

2-7 2-22. AR 600-100, "Army Leadership," 17 September 1993, 1.

2-7 Quotation from SMA Glen E. Morrell, Seventh Sergeant Major of the Army, "What Soldiering is All About," *ARMY,* Oct 1986, 41.

2-7 2-23. AR 600-20, "Army Command Policy," 13 May 2002 (hereafter cited as AR 600-20), 12.

2-8 "As a leader..." FM 22-100, *Army Leadership* (1983) (hereafter cited as FM 22-100, 1983), 89.

2-8 2-26. AR 600-20, 16.

2-8 Quotation of CSM Clifford R. West, CSM, US Army Sergeants Major Academy, 10 June 2002.

2-9 2-30. MCM, 2002, II-18.

2-11 2-34. FM 22-5, *Drill and Ceremonies,* December 1986, 7-15.

2-11 2-34. AR 1-201, "Army Inspection Policy," 17 May 1993, pp. 2-3.

2-13 "Correct errors in the use..." FM 22-10, *Leadership* (1951), 28.

2-16 2-46. FM 22-600-20, *The Army Noncommissioned Officer Guide,* November 1986 (hereafter cited as FM 22-600-20, 1986), 46.

FM 7-22.7

2-16	2-47. FM 22-600-20, 1980, 44.
2-17	2-52. AR 600-20, 12.
2-17	2-53. FM 22-600-20, 1980, pp. 17-18.
2-18	2-54. FM 22-600-20, 1986, 23.
2-18	2-55. AR 600-20, 12.
2-19	Quotation of CSM J. F. La Voie, in Ernest F. Fisher, Jr., *Guardians of the Republic* (New York, NY: Ballantine Books, 1994), 395.
2-19	2-59. DA PAM 600-25, 1987, 12.
2-21	2-62, 2-65. DA PAM 600-25, 1987, 13.
2-22	Quotation from SMA Jack L. Tilley, Twelfth Sergeant Major of the Army, "Thoughts and Concerns," Sergeant Major of the Army Website, http://www.army mil/leaders/SMA/thoughts htm.
2-22	2-69. DA PAM 600-25, 1987, 23.
2-23	2-70. FM 22-600-20, 1986, 3.

Chapter 3 – Leadership

3-2	Figure 3-1. FM 6-22, 1-3.
3-2	"Leadership is influencing…" FM 6-22, 1-4.
3-3	Quotation from SMA Robert E. Hall, Eleventh Sergeant Major of the Army, in "Keep the faith…." *The NCO Journal*, Winter 97-98, 12.
3-3	Quotation of GA Omar N. Bradley, quoted by SMA Glen E. Morrell, Seventh Sergeant Major of the Army, "NCOs Are the 'Vital Link in the Chain of Command.'" *ARMY*, Oct 1985, 65.
3-4	Quotation from MSG Frank K. Nicolas, "Noncommissioned Officer," *Infantry*, JAN 1958, 70.
3-4	Quotation from ADM James Stockdale, in address to the Graduating Class of 1979 at The Citadel, Charleston, SC; DA PAM 600-65, "Leadership Statements and Quotes," Nov 1985, 28.
3-5	Quotation from GEN John N. Abrams, "Developing Soldiers Now and into the Future" *AUSA Green Book 2001-2002*, 85.
3-5	3-9. FM 6-22, 1-6.
3-5	Quotation from GEN Matthew B. Ridgway, "Leadership," in *Military Leadership: In Pursuit of Excellence*, edited by Robert L. Taylor and William E. Rosenbach (Boulder, CO: Westview Press, Inc., 1984), 27.
3-6	Quotation from GEN Eric K. Shinseki, Chief of Staff of the Army, in an address to 25th Annual George C. Marshall ROTC Awards Seminar, Lee Chapel, Washington & Lee University, 19 April 2002.
3-6	3-14. FM 6-22, 4-13.
3-7	Quotation from LTG Harold G. Moore, US Army (retired), "Battlefield Leadership," www.lzxray.com/battle htm.
3-7	3-17. FM 1, *The Army*, 14 June 2001 (hereafter cited as FM 1), 1-1.
3-7	3-18. FM 1, 3-1.
3-8	Quotation from CSM Mary E. Sutherland, interview, 16 Sep 02.

Source Notes

3-8 Quotation from MSG (Ret) Roy Benavidez, "MSG (Ret) Roy Benavidez: A Real American Hero." *NCO Journal*, Spring 1996, 11

3-10 3-24. FM 6-22, 1-7.

3-10 Quotation from CSM Clifford West, CSM, US Army Sergeants Major Academy, 10 June 2002.

3-11 3-26. Proposed definition of mentoring, ATLDP NCO Report, para 110.

3-11 Quotation from CSM Anthony Williams, in Phil Tegtmeier, "Staying Power," *The NCO Journal*, Winter 2002, 15.

3-11 3-28. FM 6-22, 5-16.

3-12 3-31. FM 6-22, 5-19.

3-12 Quotation of SMA George W. Dunaway, Second Sergeant Major of the Army, Center of Military History Interview, 1990, 60.

3-12 3-32. FM 6-22, 5-20.

3-13 Figure 3-2. FM 6-22, 5-21.

3-14 NCO Recognition. TRADOC Regulation 600-14, "Sergeant Audie Murphy Club (SAMC) Program," 1 February 1999, 12.

3-14 3-33. FM 1, 3-1.

3-14 Quotation of LTG McNair by GEN Eisenhower, DA PAM 600-65, 7.

3-14 "The discipline on which..." The Old Sergeant's Conferences, 1930, 64.

3-15 "Men like to serve..." TGGS Special Text No. 1, *Leadership for the Company Officer*, (1949), 144.

3-15 3-36. AR 600-20, 15.

3-15 **C Company, 3-504th PIR at Renacer Prison**, Center for Army Lessons Learned, *Combat Training Center Bulletin*, September 1990, 4-1.

3-16 Quotation from GEN George S. Patton, Sr., "3rd US Army Letter of Instruction No. 2," 3 April 1944.

3-16 **The Deployment**, Center for Army Lessons Learned, *Newsletter*, Sep 1993, 2.

3-17 3-42. FM 6-22, 3-18.

3-17 Quotation from LTG William M. Steele, "Training and Developing Army Leaders," *Military Review*, July-August 2001.

3-17 3-43. FM 6-22, 1-9.

3-18 Quotation from SMA Julius Gates, Eighth Sergeant Major of the Army, "NCOs: Maintain the Momentum." *Field Artillery*, Dec 1987, 46.

Chapter 4 – Training

4-1 "Noncommissioned officers train soldiers..." FM 25-101, *Battle Focused Training*, Sep 1990 (hereafter cited as FM 25-101), 3-1.

4-3 Quotation from CSM A. Frank Lever, III, interview, 30 Sep 02.

4-4 Quotation from SGT Michael Davis, "Sergeants on Training." *Sergeants' Business*, Jul-Aug 1988, 13.

4-6 Figure 4-1. FM 25-101, 3.

4-6 **Corporal Sandy Jones in World War I**, in Laurence Stallings, *The Doughboys: The Story of the AEF* (New York, NY: Harper & Row, 1963), 318.

FM 7-22.7

4-7	Quotation from CSM Bobby Butler, "Iron Time Training." *Army Trainer*, Fall 1989, 9.
4-9	Quotation from SSG Ray H. Duncan, "The Value of Military Training." *US Army Recruiting News*, 1 March 1925, 12.
4-10	**The 555th Parachute Infantry – 'Triple Nickles,'** in Bradley Biggs, *The Triple Nickles*, Archon Books, an imprint of The Shoe String Press, Inc. Hamden, Connecticut, 1986.
4-11	Quotation from SMA William O. Wooldridge, First Sergeant Major of the Army, "So You're Headed for Combat." *Army Digest*, Jan 1968, pp. 6-11.
4-11	Quotation of SFC Lydia Mead, *The NCO Journal*, Spring 1993, 6.
4-12	Quotation from MSG Jose R. Carmona, "Only a Trained Instructor Can Teach." *ARMY*, Jan 1968, 74.
4-12	Quotation of CSM Mary E. Sutherland, interview, 16 Sep 02.
4-13	"Carefully planned, purposeful and effective training…" DA Pam 22-1, *Leadership* (1948), 33.
4-15	**SSG Michael Duda in Desert Storm**, in Center for Army Lessons Learned, "Vignette: Operation Desert Storm: Actions on Day G + 3," *CALL Newsletter 92-4*, October 1992.
4-16	Quotation from SSG Rico Johnston, "Battle Drills." *Army Trainer*, Fall 1981, 14.
4-17	4-47. AAR Steps from TC 25-20, *A Leader's Guide to After-Action Reviews*, 30 Sep 93, 4.
4-17	"AARs are one of the best…" Center for Army Lessons Learned, *NCO Lessons Learned*, Oct 1989, 11.
4-18	4-51. Platoon Training Meeting Agenda from TC 25-30, *A Leader's Guide to Company Training Meetings*, 27 Apr 94, (hereafter cited as TC 25-30), 12.

Chapter 5 – Counseling and Mentorship

5-3	5-3. Requirement for counseling in AR 600-20, 6.
5-4	Quotation from CSM Anthony Williams, in Phil Tegtmeier, "Staying Power," *The NCO Journal*, Winter 2002, 15.
5-4	Figure 5-1. FM 6-22, C-2.
5-5	Quotation from CSM Daniel E. Wright, "Tips for Leaders." *Field Artillery*, Jun 1995, 3.
5-6	Quotation from COL David Reaney, *Command, Leadership and Effective Staff Support*, 1996, 159.
5-6	Figure 5-2. FM 6-22, C-17.
5-7	Quotation from SGM Randolph Hollinsworth, in *The NCO Corps on Leadership, the Army and America: Quotes for Winners*, 2nd Ed. (Washington DC: The Information Management Support Center, January 1998), 18.
5-10	"[Helping] soldiers cope with…" FM 22-600-20, 1980, pp. 33, 35.
5-11	"Performance counseling informs…" DA Pam 623-205, "The NCO Evaluation Reporting System 'In Brief,'" 1988, 6.
5-12	5-28. AR 623-205, "Noncommissioned Officer Evaluation Reporting System," 15 May 2002, 3.

Source Notes-6

Source Notes

5-16 Quotation from CSM A. Frank Lever, III, interview, 30 Sep 02.

5-16 "To be an effective mentor..." DA Pam 600-25, 18.

5-16 "One of the most important..." CSM Larry W. Gammon, "The Mentor and Mentoring." *Quartermaster Professional Bulletin*, Spring 2001.

5-17 Figure 5-4. DA PAM 600-XX (Draft), "Army Mentorship," undated.

5-17 Quotation of CSM Cynthia A. Pritchett, in Patrick A. Swan, "'Knowledge Warriors' amass at Symposium." *ArmyLink News*, 4 April, 2002.

5-18 Figure 5-5. CSM Christine E. Seitzinger, "NCO Mentorship." *The NCO Journal Online*, Fall 1997.

5-18 Quotation from SMA William G. Bainbridge, Fifth Sergeant Major of the Army *Top Sergeant: The Life and Times of Sergeant Major of the Army William G. Bainbridge,* (New York, NY: Ballantine Books, 1995), 346.

5-19 Quotation from CSM Christine E. Seitzinger, "NCO Mentorship." *The NCO Journal Online*, Fall 1997.

Appendix A – Sergeant's Time Training

A-1 Quotation from GEN Eric K. Shinseki, in SSG Tami Lambert, "GEN Shinseki promoted to NCO," PAO, HQUSAREUR, US Army Europe News Release, October 2000.

Appendix B – Army Programs

B-2 Quotation from SMA Silas L. Copeland, Third Sergeant Major of the Army, "Let's Build a Better Army," *Soldier*, Jul 1971, 5.

B-6 Quotation from MSG Douglas E. Freed, "Learning to Lead," *Army Trainer*, Fall 1987, 30.

Appendix C – Leader Book

C-1 C-4. Organization of the leader book from TC 25-30, B-3.

Appendix F – NCO Induction Ceremony

F-1 F-1. The ceremony outline shown here developed by CSM Dan Elder by melding many Army units' versions, http://www.squad-leader.com.

F-1 Quotation form SMA William G. Bainbridge, Fifth Sergeant Major of the Army, "First and Getting Firster," *Army*, Oct 1975, 24.

F-4 Quotation from CSM Joshua Perry, "Regimental Command Sergeant Major," *Military Police*, Dec 1990, 5.

F-5 **History of the NCO Creed** from CSM Dan Elder and CSM Felix Sanchez, "The History of the NCO Creed," *NCO Journal*, Summer 1998.

FM 7-22.7

Source Notes-8

Glossary

The glossary list acronyms and abbreviations used in this manual. AR 310-50 lists authorized abbreviations and brevity codes.

1SG	First Sergeant
AAR	After-Action Review
AC	Active Component
ACES	Army Continuing Education System
ACAP	Army Career and Alumni Program
ACCP	Army Correspondence Course Program
ACS	Army Community Service
ACT	American College Test
ADM	Admiral
AER	Army Emergency Relief
AFAP	Army Family Action Plan
AFTB	Army Family Team Building
AKO	Army Knowledge Online
APFT	Army Physical Fitness Program
ANCOC	Advance Noncommissioned Officers Course
AR	Army Regulation
ARNG	Army National Guard
ARTEP	Army Training Evaluation Program
ARTEP MTP	Army Training Evaluation Program Mission Training Plan
ASAP	Army Substance Abuse Program
AT	Annual Training
ATLS	Advanced Trauma Life Support
ATRRS	Army Training and Requirements Resource System
AWOL	absent without leave
BARS	BNCOC Automated Reservation System
BNCOC	Basic Noncommissioned Officers Course
BOSS	Better Opportunities for Single Soldiers
BSB	Base Support Battalion
BSC	Battle Staff Course
CA	Combat Arms
CAFAP	Consumer Affairs and Financial Assistance Program
CLEP	College Level Examination Program
CMF	Career Management Field
COL	Colonel
CPL	Corporal
CQ	Charge of Quarters
CS	Combat Support
CSM	Command Sergeant Major
CSMC	Command Sergeant Major Course
CSS	Combat Service Support
CTT	Common Task Testing
CW2	Chief Warrant Officer 2
DA	Department of the Army
DANTES	Defense Activity for Non-Traditional Education Support
DA PAM	Department of the Army Pamphlet

Glossary-1

D-Day	Execution Date of Any Military Operation
DOD	Department of Defense
DOR	Date of Rank
DWI	Driving while intoxicated
EEO	Equal Employment Opportunity
EFMP	Exceptional Family Member Program
EO	Equal Opportunity
EPMS	Enlisted Personnel Management System
FAP	Family Advocacy Program
FM	Field Manual
FMEAP	Family Member Employment Assistance Program
FRAGO	Fragmentary Order
FRG	Family Readiness Group
FSC	First Sergeant Course
FTX	Field Training Exercise
GEN	General
HMMWV	High Mobility Medium Wheeled Vehicle
IAW	In Accordance With
ID	Identification
LDP	Leader Development Program
LTG	Lieutenant General
LZ	Landing Zone
MACOM	Major Army Command
MCM	Manual for Courts Martial
MEDEVAC	Medical Evacuation
METL	Mission Essential Task List
METT-TC	Mission, Enemy, Terrain, Troops, Time and Civilian Considerations
MILES	Multiple Integrated Laser Engagement System
MKT	Mobile Kitchen Trailer
MOS	Military Occupational Specialty
MSG	Master Sergeant
MTP	Mission Training Plan
MWR	Moral, Welfare, and Recreation
NATO	North Atlantic Treaty Organization
NBC	Nuclear Biological Chemical
NCO	Noncommissioned Officer
NCOA	Noncommissioned Officer Academy
NCODP	Noncommissioned Officer Development Program
NCOER	Noncommissioned Officer Evaluation Report
NCOERS	Noncommissioned Officer Evaluation Reporting System
NCOES	Noncommissioned Officer Education System
NCOIC	Noncommissioned Officer In-Charge
NCOPD	Noncommissioned Officer Professional Development
NMC	Nonmission Capable
OC	Observer Controller
OCOKA	Observation, Concealment, Obstacles, Key terrain, Avenues of approach
ODCSOPS	Office of the Deputy Chief of Operations
ODSCPER	Office of the Deputy Chief of Staff Personnel

Glossary

OOTW	Operations Other Than War
OPFOR	Opposing Forces
OPORD	Operation Order
"P"	Needs Practice
(P)	Promotable
PCC	Pre-combat Checks
PCI	Pre-combat Inspections
PDF	Panamanian Defense Force
PDM	Professional Development Model
PERSCOM	Personnel Command
PFC	Private First Class
PIR	Parachute Infantry Regiment
PLDC	Primary Leadership Development Course
PLT	Platoon
PMCS	Preventive Maintenance Checks and Services
PMOS	Primary Military Occupational Specialty
POV	Privately Owned Vehicle
PSG	Platoon Sergeant
PZ	Pickup Zone
QOL	Quality of Life
RAP	Relocation Assistance Program
RC	Reserve Component
Ret.	Retired
SAT	Scholastic Assessment Test
SATS	Standard Army Training System
SFC	Sergeant First Class
SGM	Sergeant Major
SGT	Sergeant
SMA	Sergeant Major of the Army
SMC	Sergeants Major Course
SOP	Standing Operating Procedure
SPC	Specialist
SSG	Staff Sergeant
STP	Soldier Training Publication
STT	Sergeants Time Training
"T"	Trained
TA	Tuition Assistance
TABE	Test of Adult Basic Education
TADSS	Training Aids, Devices, Simulators, and Simulations
TAO	Transition Assistance Office
TAPES	Total Army Performance Evaluation System
TIG	Time in Grade
TIS	Time in Service
TOW	Tube Launched, Optically Tracked, Wire-Guided Missile
TM	Technical Manual
TRADOC	US Army Training and Doctrine Command
TTP	Tactics, Techniques, and Procedures
T&EO	Training and Evaluation Outline
"U"	Untrained
UCMJ	Uniform Code of Military Justice

UN	United Nations
US	United States
USAR	United States Army Reserve
USASMC	United States Army Sergeants Major Course
USC	United States Code
VIP	Very Important Person
WARNORD	Warning Order
WO1	Warrant Officer 1
WWI	World War 1
WWII	World War 2

Bibliography

The bibliography lists field manuals by new number followed by old number. These publications are sources for additional information on the topics in this Field Manual.

JOINT PUBLICATIONS

Most joint publications are available online at http://www.dtic.mil/doctrine/jel/

Joint Doctrine Encyclopedia. 16 Jul.1997.

ARMY PUBLICATIONS

Most Army doctrinal publications are available online at the Reimer Digital Library (http://155.217.58.58/atdls htm).

ARMY REGULATIONS (AR)

AR 27-10. *Military Justice*. 20 Aug 1999.
AR 310-25. *Dictionary of United States Army Terms*. 21 May 1986.
AR 600-20. *Army Command Policy*. 15 Jul 1999.
AR 600-100. *Army Leadership*. 17 Sep 1993.
AR 635-200. *Enlisted Personnel*. 26 Jan 1996.
AR 690-600. *Equal Employment Opportunity Discrimination Complaints*. 18 Sep 1989.
AR 690-950. *Career Management*. 18 Aug 1988.

DEPARTMENT OF THE ARMY PAMPHLETS (DA PAM)

DA Pam 10-1. *Organization of the US Army*. 14 Jun 1994.
DA Pam 350-58. *Leader Development of America's Army*. 13 Oct 1994.
DA Pam 350-59. *Army Correspondence Course Program Catalog*. 1 Oct 2000.
DA Pam 600-25. *US Army Noncommissioned Officer Professional Development Guide*. 30 Apr 1987.
DA Pam 623-205. *The Noncommissioned Officer Evaluation Reporting System*. 29 Jun 1988.
DA Pam 690-400. *Total Army Performance Evaluation System (TAPES)*. 1 Jun 1993.

FIELD MANUALS (FM)

FM 1 (100-1). *The Army*. 14 Jun 1994.
FM 1-04.10 (27-10). *The Law of Land Warfare*. 15 Jul 1976.
FM 2-22.4 (34-54). *Counterintelligence*. 30 Jan 1998.
FM 3-0 (100-5). *Operations*. 14 Jun 2001.
FM 3-05.30 (33-1). *Psychological Operations*. 19 Jun 2000.
FM 3-05.40 (41-10). *Civil Affairs Operations*. 14 Feb 2000.

FM 3-05.70 (21-31). *Survival.* 5 Jan 1992.
FM 3-07.2 (100-35). *Force Protection.* TBP.
FM 3-07.3 (100-23). *Peace Operations.* 30 Dec 1994.
FM 3-07.7 (100-19). *Domestic Support Operations.* 1 Jul 1993.
FM 3-11.19 (3-19). *NBC Reconnaissance.* 19 Nov 1993.
FM 3-11.4 (3-4). *NBC Protection.* 21 Feb 1996.
FM 3-11.5 (3-5). *NBC Decontamination.* 17 Nov 1993.
FM 3-11.7 (3-7). *NBC Field Handbook.* 29 Sep 1994.
FM 3-19.30 (19-30). *Physical Security.* 8 Jan 2001.
FM 3-2 (21-20). *Physical Fitness Training.* 1 Oct 1998.
FM 3-21.18 (21-18). *Foot Marches.* 1 Jun 1990.
FM 3-21.5 (22-5). *Drill and Ceremonies.* 8 Dec 1986.
FM 3-21.6 (22-6). *Guard Duty.* 15 Jan 1975.
FM 3-21.75 (21-75). *Combat Skills of the Soldier.* 3 Aug 1984.
FM 3-25.26 (21-26). *Map Reading and Land Navigation.* 20 Jul 2001.
FM 3-34.1 (5-102). *Countermobility.* 14 Mar 1985.
FM 3-34.112 (5-103). *Survivability.* 10 Jun 1985.
FM 3-34.330 (5-33). *Terrain Analysis.* 8 Sep 1992.
FM 3-35 (100-17). *Mobilization, Deployment, Redeployment and Demobilization.* 28 Oct 1992.
FM 3-35.5 (100-17-5). *Redeployment.* 29 Sep 1999.
FM 3-97.11 (90-11). *Cold Weather Operations.* 12 Apr 1968.
FM 3-100.14 (100-14). *Risk Management.* 23 Apr 1998.
FM 4-0 (100-10). *Combat Service Support.* 3 Oct 1995.
FM 4-01.30 (55-10). *Movement Control.* 9 Feb 1999.
FM 4-02.51 (8-51). *Combat Stress Control in Theater Operations.* 29 Sep 1994.
FM 4-25.10 (21-10). *Field Hygiene and Sanitation.* 21 Jun 2000.
FM 4-25.11 (21-11). *First Aid for Soldiers.* 27 Oct 1988.
FM 4-25.12 (21-10-1). *Unit Field Sanitation Team.* 25 Jan 2002.
FM 4-100.9 (100-9). *Reconstitution.* 13 Jan 1992.
FM 5-0 (101-5). *Staff Organization and Operations.* 31 May 1997.
FM 6-22 (22-100). *Army Leadership.* 31 Aug 1999.
FM 6-22.5 (22-9). *Combat Stress.* 23 Jun 2000.
FM 7-0. *Training the Force.* 21 Oct 2002.
FM 7-1 (25-101). *Battle Focus Training.* 30 Sep 1990.
FM 7-15. *Army Universal Task List (AUTL).* TBP.
FM 22-9. *Soldier's Performance in Continuous Operations.* 12 Dec 1991.
FM 22-51. *Leader's Manual for Combat Stress Control.* 29 Sep 1994.
FM 27-14. *Legal Guide for Soldiers.* 16 Apr 1991.
FM 101-5-1. *Operational Terms and Graphics.* 30 Sep 1997.

SOLDIER TRAINING PUBLICATIONS (STP)

STP 21-1 SMCT. *Soldiers Manual of Common Tasks, Skill Level 1*. Oct 2002.

STP 21-24-SMCT. *Soldiers Manual of Common Tasks, Skill Levels 2-4*. Oct 2002.

TRAINING CIRCULARS (TC)

TC 21-3. *Soldier's Handbook for Individual Operations and Survival in Cold-Weather Areas*. 17 Mar 1986.

TC 21-7. *Personal Financial Readiness and Deployment Handbook*. 17 Nov 1997.

TC 25-10. *A Leader's Guide to Lane Training*. 26 Aug 1996.

TC 25-20. *A Leader's Guide to After-Action Reviews*. 30 Sep 1993.

TC 25-30. *A Leader's Guide to Company Training Meetings*. 27 Apr 1994.

TC 90-1. *Training in Urban Operations*. 1 Apr 2002.

US ARMY TRAINING AND DOCTRINE COMMAND PUBLICATIONS

TRADOC Reg 350-10. *Institutional Leader Educational Training*. 12 Aug 2002.

TRADOC Reg 350-18. *The Army School System (TASS)*. 28 May 2000.

TRADOC Pam 525-5. *Force XXI Operations*. 1 Aug 1994.

TRADOC Pam 525-100-4. *Leadership and Command on the Battlefield, Noncommissioned Officer Corps*. 28 Feb 1994.

MISCELLANEOUS GOVERNMENT PUBLICATIONS

MCM. *Manual for Courts Martial United States*. 2002.

FM 7-22.7

Index

Entries are by paragraph numbers unless page is specified

54th Massachusetts Regiment, page 1-8
555th Parachute Infantry, page 4-12

A

AAR, 4-46
    Four Parts, 4-47
Abrams, GEN John N., pages 1-22, 3-5
Abstract of Infantry Tactics, 1-9
Afghanistan, 1-41, pages, 1-3, 1-21
Al Qaeda, 1-41
Alcohol and Drug Control Officer, B-5
Adjutant, 1-10
American College Test (ACT), 1-71f
American Revolution, 1-3- 1-6
ANCOC, 1-63
Army Birthday, page 1-1
Army Counseling Program, 5-8
    Effective 5-8
    Four Elements, 5-8
    Characteristics of Effective
    Counseling, 5-7 (fig 5-1)
    Assess the Plan of Action, 5-10
Army Career and Alumni Program, (ACAP) B-2
Army Community Service (ACS), B-15
Army Continuing Education system (ACES), 1-71, B-4
Army Correspondence Course Program (ACCP), 1-71j
Army Emergency Relief (AER), B-8
Army Knowledge Online (AKO), 1-71b,
Army Leadership, 3-4
Army Leadership Framework, 3-43 (fig 3-1)
Army Programs, B-1
    Transition Assistance, B-2
    Equal Opportunity/Equal Employment Opportunity (EO/EEO), B-3
    Education, B-4
    Army Substance Abuse Program (ASAP), B-5--B-7
    Army Emergency Relief (AER), B-8

Army Regulation (AR) 600-20, B-3
Army Regulation (AR) 600-85, B-8
Army Regulation (AR), 690-600, B-4
Army Training and Education Program, 1-59 (fig 1-1)
Army Transformation, 1-48
Army Values, 1-50 -- 1-58
Army Women, 1-28
Ashley, SFC Eugene, page 1-15
Assessments, 4-42
    Leader, 4-42
    Unit, 4-43
    Tools, 4-45
        Leader Book, 4-45
        Battle Rosters, 4-45
Army Training Requirement and Resources System (ATRRS), 1-71a
Authority, 2-19-- 2-21
    Types, 2-21
    Command 2-22- 2-23
    General Military, 2-24-- 2-26
    Delegation of Authority, 2-27-- 2-31
    Types of Sources, 2-27-- 2-29

B

Badge of Military Merit, 1-7
Backbone of the Army, 2-46, F-10
Bainbridge, SMA William G., page 5-18
Balkans, The, 1-40
Basic Noncommissioned Officer Course (BNCOC), 1-61
Battle Drills, 4-40
    Characteristics of, 4-40
Battle Focus Training, 4-4
Battle Staff Course (BSC), 1-34
Be, Know, Do, 3-6-- 3-32
    Be, 3-7-- 3-9
    Know, 3-10-- 3-19
    Do 3-20-- 3-32
Benavidez, MSG (USA Ret) Roy (MOH), page 3-8
Better Opportunities for Single Soldiers (BOSS), B-14

FM 7-22.7

Blue Book, 1-3
BNCOC Automated Reservation System (BARS), 1-62
Bradley, General of the Army Omar N., page 1-24, 3-33
Brown, Sergeant William, page 1-5
Buffalo Soldier, page 1-9
    Sergeant George Jordan, page 1-9

C

C Co. 3-504th PIR, page 3-16
Camp Bondsteel, page 1-7
Career Management Field (CMF), 1-71f
Carney, Sergeant William H., page 1-8
Center for Army Lessons Learned (CALL), page 4-17
Chain of Command, 2-20, 2-28, 2-35, 2-39, 2-48, 2-50, 2-53, 4-7, 4-19, 4-35, 5-15, 5-21, pages 3-7, 3-9, 3-10
Character, 3-6-- 3-7
Chevrons, 1-21
Chief of Staff Intent, STT, A-1
Civil War, 1-11
    Post Civil War Era 1-14
Colors and Color Guards, pages 2-20-- 2-21
    CSM Responsibility, pages 2-20-- 2-21
    Color Sergeant, pages 2-20-- 2-21
Commander's Assessment, 4-42
Command Sergeant Major and Sergeant Major, 2-59-- 2-61
Command Authority, 2-22
Command Responsibility, 2-16
Command Sergeants Major Course (CSMC), 1-34
Commissioned Officers Duties, 2-42 (fig 2-5)
Common Task Test Proficiency, C-7
Congress, 1-19, 2-20, 2-27
Connelly, SMA William, page 1-25
Constitution, 1-50, 2-20, 2-28,
Containment, 1-32
Contemporary Ops Environment, 1-43, 1-44, 1-45
Continental Army, pages 1-1- 1-4
Copeland, SMA Silas L., page B-2
Corporal Titus, page 1-9

Counseling and Mentorship, 5-1
Counseling 5-2
    Definition, 5-2
Counseling Process, 5-9
    Four Stages, 5-9
Counseling Session Example, pages 5-13-- 5-15, 5-20
Counseling Styles, 5-7
    Characteristics, 5-7 (fig 5-1)
Courage, 1-57, 3-16, 5-6,
Crew Drills, 4-41

D

D-Day, 6 June 1944, 1-27
Defense Activity for Non-Traditional Education Support (DANTES), 1-71
Deployment, The, page 3-16
Developmental Counseling, 5-11--5-21
    Types, 5-11
    Major Aspects of, fig 5-2
    Event Oriented, 5-12
    Counseling For Specific Instances, 5-13
    Action Taken, 5-14
    Reception and Integration, 5-15
    Counseling Points, fig 5-3
    Crisis Counseling, 5-16
    Referral Counseling, 5-17, 5-18
    Promotion Counseling, 5-19
    Adverse Separation Counseling 5-20
Discipline, 3-33-- 3-38, page 3-15--3-16
Douglass, Frederick, page 1-8
Drills, 4-38--4-39
    Types, 4-39
Duda, Staff Sergeant Michael, page 4-15
Dunaway, SMA George W., page 3-12
Duties of Commissioned Officers, 2-42 (fig 2-5)
Duties of NCOs (Von Steuben), 1-4, 2-46 (fig 2-7)
Duties of Warrant Officers, 2-46 (fig 2-6)
Duties, Responsibility, and Authority, 2-5
Duty, 2-6
    Types, 2-10
Specified, 2-11

Index

Directed, 2-12
Implied, 2-13

E

Enlisted Retirement, 1-19
Education, 1-29, 1-34, 1-59, 1-60, 1-70, 5-8,
Equal Employment Opportunity, B-4
Equal Opportunity, B-3
Essential Soldier Task Proficiency, pages C-8
Event Oriented Counseling, 5-12
    Examples, 5-12

F

Fieldcraft Know, 3-13
Field Manual 22-100, page 5-2
Field Officer, 1-10
First Sergeant Course (FSC), 1-34
Floyd, Sergeant Charles, page xii
Freed, MSG Douglas E., page B-6
Full Spectrum Operations, 1-42

G

Gammon, CSM Larry W., page 5-16
Gass, Sergeant Patrick, page xii
Gates, SMA, Julius W., page 3-18
General Military Authority, 2-24
Grenada, 1-36
Gordon, Master Sergeant Gary I., page 1-18
Gulf War, The, 1-37

H

Haiti, 1-39
Hall, SMA Robert E., page 3-3
Hayes, President Rutherford B., page 1-7
Hernandez, Corporal Rodolfo P., page 1-25
History of the NCO Creed, page F-5
Hollingsworth, SGM Randolph S, page 5-7

I

Ia Drang Valley, 1-1

Individual Responsibility, 2-18
Individual Training, 4-3
Information Environment, 1-46
Inspections and Corrections, 2-32-- 2-33
    Types, 2-34
    First Line Leaders, 2-33
Intended and Unintended Consequences, 3-39-- 3-42
Internet Resources List, page D-1
Institutional Training, 1-59- 1-64
Integrated Army, 1-30

J

Jones, Corporal Sandy E., page 4-6
Jordan, Sergeant George, page 1-9

K

Kidd, SMA Richard A., page 2-7
Korea, 1-30
Kosovo, 1-40
Kuwait, 1-37

L

La Voie, CSM J. F., page 2-19
Lang Vei, page 1-15
Leader Concerns in Training 4-33-- 4-34
Leader Development Process, 1-59
    Three Pillars, 1-59
Leader's Responsibility, 4-5
Leader Book, C-1
    Example forms, pages C-6-- C-24
Leaders' Role in Training, 4-15-- 4-16
    Exchange Information, 4-15
    Demand Soldiers Achieve Training Standards, 4-15
    Assess the Results in the AAR, 4-15
    Planning, 4-17-- 4-21
        Short Range, 4-17
    Preparation, 4-22-- 4-27
    Execution, 4-28
    Standards, 4-32
Leadership, 3-1
    First Line of, 3-2
    Learned, 3-4
    Attributes, 3-6

FM 7-22.7

    Be, 3-7-- 3-9
    Know, 3-10-- 3-19
    Do 3-20-- 3-32
Leadership Positions, page 2-3
    Assuming, 2-1, (fig 2-1), 2-3
    (fig 2-2)
Lever, CSM A. Frank III, pages 4-3, 5-16
Lewis and Clark Expedition, page xii
Little Round Top, 1-1
Littrell, CSM (USA Ret) Gary L., pages ix - xi
Lowe, Percival, page 1-6
Lundy's Lane, page xii

M

Master Sergeant, 2-62
McKinley, President William, page 1-7
Medal of Honor, page xi
Mentorship, 5-33
    Defined, 5-33
    Effective Mentor, 5-34
    Developmental Relationship, 5-35
    Development Model (fig 5-4)
    Sustain Mentorship, 5-37
    Characteristics, 5-38 (fig 5-5)
    Of Officers, 5-39
    Building of the Future, 5-40
Military Life on the Frontier, 1-15
    Marriages, 1-16
    Barracks, 1-17
    Handbooks, 1-17
    Pay, 1-18
Mission, Enemy, Terrain, Troops, and Time (METT-T), 4-39
Mission Essential Task List (METL), 4-3-- 4-6
    Battle Focus, 4-4
    Collective Task, 4-3
    Individual Training, 4-3
    Leader/Soldier Task Selection, 4-10
METL Crosswalk, 4-6
METL Integration, 4-7
    Platoon, Squad Collective Task, 4-8
    STP, MTP, SM, 4-12
    Planning, 4-17-- 4-21
        Short Range, 4-17
        Long Range, 4-17
        Near Term Planning, 4-19
    Preparation, 4-22-- 4-27
    Training Assessment, 4-42
    Training Execution, 4-28
    Training Meetings, 4-18
        Battalion/Company, 4-18
        Platoon/Squad/Section, 4-19
    Training Preparation, 4-22-- 4-24
    Training Schedules, 4-20
        Approval, 4-20
        Signature, 4-20
    Task Approval Matrix, 4-12, (fig 4)
Mize, Sergeant Ola L., page 1-14
Mock, CSM George D., page 1-29
Mogadishu, 1-1, page 1-18
Monte Damiano, Italy, 1-27
Morale, Welfare, and Recreation (MWR), page B-17
Morrell, SMA Glen E., page 2-7
Multiple Integrated Laser Engagement System (MILES), 4-23

N

NCO
    Charge, page vii
    Creed, Back Cover
    Duties, 2-46 (fig 2-7)
    Education, 1-29, 1-34
    Education System (NCOES), 1-60-- 1-64
    Evaluation Report (NCOER), 5-26- 5-28
    History, 1-1
    Induction Ceremony Sample, F-1
    Manual, 1909, 1-20
    Mentorship of Officers, 5-39
    Primary Trainer Responsibility, 4-30
    Professional Development, 1-59
    Reading List, page E-1
    Recognition, page 3-14
    Role in Training, 4-53
    Transition, page 1-32
    Vision, page viii
NCO Ranks, 2-57-- 2-70
    Sergeant Major of the Army, 2-57-- 2-58

Index

Command Sergeant Major and Sergeant Major, 2-59-- 2-61
First Sergeant and Master Sergeant, 2-62-- 2-64
Platoon Sergeant and Sergeant First Class, 2-65-- 2-67
Section, Squad and Team Leaders, 2-68-- 2-69
NCO Ranks Insignia, 1-8-- 1-10
  Modern, 1-21
NCO Support Channel, 2-50-- 2-56
  In Addition, 2-52
  Assist Chain of Command, 2-55
NCO's Make It Happen, 4-29
Noncommissioned, Commissioned, and Warrant Officer Relationship, 2-41-- 2-46
Noncommissioned Officer Development Program (NCODP), 1-67

O

Omaha Beach, 1-1
On The Spot Corrections, 2-35
  Guidelines, fig 2-3
  Steps, fig 2-4
On The Spot Inspections, 2-38
  Steps, 2-38
On The Spot Praise, 2-36
Operation
  Allied Force, 1-40
  Anaconda, 1-41
  Desert Storm, 1-37
  Enduring Freedom, 1-41
  Just Cause, 1-36
  Restore Hope, 1-38
  Support Hope, 1-38
  Uphold Democracy, 1-39
  Urgent Fury, 1-36
Operational Assignments, 1-59
Opportunity Training, 4-37
Otani, Staff Sergeant Kazuo, page 1-12
Outpost Harry, page 1-14

P

Panama, 1-36
Park, Sergeant, page 2-13
Performance and Professional Growth Counseling, 5-22
  Performance, 5-22-- 5-25
  Professional Growth, 5-29-- 5-32
Platoon Sergeant and Sergeant First Class, 2-65-- 2-67
Primary Leadership Development Course (PLDC), 1-60
Pre-Combat Checks (PCCs), 2-39
Pre-Combat Inspections (PCIs), 2-39
Pre-Execution Checks, 2-39
Pritchett, CSM Cynthia A., pages 1-4, 5-17
Pride, 3-33
Professional Development Models (PDM), 1-71
Purple Heart, 1-7
Pusan Perimeter, page 1-3
Putting It Together, 3-43-- 3-44

Q

Quality Of Life Programs (QOL), B-11
  Army Sponsorship, B-12
  Better Opportunities For Single Soldiers (BOSS), B-13
  American Red Cross, B-14
  Army Community Service (ACS), B-15
  Morale, Welfare, and Recreation (MWR), B-16
  Family Readiness Groups (FRG), B-17
  Resources, B-17

R

Regulations, 1-3, 1-16, 2-29
Regulations for the Order and Discipline of Troops of the United States, 1-3
Responsibility, 2-14-- 2-15
  Command, 2-16-- 2-17
  Individual, 2-18
Realism, Training, 4-33
Reading List, page E-1
  Recommended Professional Reading List for NCOs, page E-1
Revolution, 1-3
Risk Assessment, 4-35
  Assessment Card, pages C-22, C-23
Rissler, Sergeant James R., page xiii

FM 7-22.7

Roberts, Sergeant Christine, page 1-20
Rwanda, 1-1, 1-38

S

Safety, 4-35
Scholastic Assessment Test (SAT), 1-71f
Section, Squad and Team Leader, 2-68-- 2-69
Selection of collective Task, 4-6
Self-Development, 1-68- 1-69
    Education Activities to Support, 1-70
Self-awareness, 3-17
Self-confidence, 3-16
Senior NCO Responsibility in Training, 4-1
Serbia, 1-40
Sergeant Audie Murphy Club, page 3-14
Sergeant First Class, 2-66
Sergeant Major, 2-61
Sergeant Major of the Army, 1-33, 2-57-- 2-58
Sergeant Morales Club, page 3-14
Sergeant's Time Training, 4-35, A-1-- A-5
    NCO Responsibilities, A-6-- A-8
    Do's and Don'ts, A-9
    A Technique, A-10-- A-16
STT Books, A-15
STT Equipment, A-16
STT Timeline, A-17
Supervisor's Sergeant's Time Book, A-11
Shahi-Kot, page xiii
Shinseki, GEN Eric K., pages 3-6, and A-1
Shughart, Sergeant First Class Randall D., page 1-18
Sjogren, Staff Sergeant John, page 1-13
Somalia, 1-38
Special Mention Positions, 2-47-- 2-49
    Platoon Sergeant, 2-47
    Squad, Section, and Team Leader, 2-48
St. Mihiel, 1-1
Standard Army Training System (SATS), C-9
Standards in Training, 4-32

Sutherland, CSM Mary E., pages 3-8, 4-12

T

Tactics, Techniques and Procedures (TTP), 4-39
Taliban, 1-41
Team Building Stages, 3-31, page 3-13, (fig 3-2)
Test of Adult Basic Education (TABE), 1-71f
Three Pillars of NCOPD, The, 1-59
Tilley, SMA Jack L., pages viii, 1-22, 2-22,
Titus, Musician Corporal Calvin P., page 1-9
Training, page 4-1
    NCO's Role, 4-1
Training Aids, Devices, Simulator and Simulations (TADSS), 4-23
Training Assessment, 4-42
Training Meetings, 4-48-- 4-53
    Battalion/Companies, 4-47
    Platoon, 4-48-- 4-51
Training Preparation, 4-21
    Rehearse, 4-21
    Review, 4-21
Transition Assistance Office (TAO), B-2
Triple Nickles, (The 555th Parachute Infantry), page 4-10
Tools, 4-42
Troop Leading Procedures, 3-22
    Outline, pages C-18-- C-20
Tuition Assistance (TA), 1-71e

U

US Army Sergeants Major Course (USASMC), 1-64

V

Valley Forge, 1-1
Van Autreve, Fourth SMA Leon L. page 2-5
Vietnam, 1-32
Von Steuben, Baron Friedrich, 1-3, 1-20, 1-35, 5-1, F-10

W

Walsh, Sergeant Patrick, page 1-11
Warrior ethos, 1-58
West, Clifford R., pages 2-8, 3-10
Williams, CSM Anthony, pages 3-11, 5-4

X - Y - Z

Yugoslavia, 1-40

Notes

Notes

Notes

Notes

Notes

Notes

FM 7-22.7 (TC 22-6)
23 DECEMBER 2002

By order of the Secretary of the Army:

ERIC K. SHINSEKI
General, United States Army
Chief of Staff

Official:

JOEL B. HUDSON
Administrative Assistant to the
Secretary of the Army
0233102

DISTRIBUTION:

Active Army, Army National Guard, and US Army Reserve: To be distributed in accordance with the initial distribution number 111058, requirements for
FM 7-22.7.

Creed of the Noncommissioned Officer

No one is more professional than I. I am a Noncommissioned Officer, a leader of soldiers. As a noncommissioned officer, I realize that I am a member of a time honored corps, which is known as "the Backbone of the Army." I am proud of the Corps of Noncommissioned Officers and will at all times conduct myself so as to bring credit upon the Corps, the military service and my country regardless of the situation in which I find myself. I will not use my grade or position to attain pleasure, profit or personal safety.

Competence is my watch-word. My two basic responsibilities will always be uppermost in my mind – accomplishment of my mission and the welfare of my soldiers. I will strive to remain technically and tactically proficient. I am aware of my role as a noncommissioned officer. I will fulfill my responsibilities inherent in that role. All soldiers are entitled to outstanding leadership; I will provide that leadership. I know my soldiers and I will always place their needs above my own. I will communicate consistently with my soldiers and never leave them uninformed. I will be fair and impartial when recommending both rewards and punishment.

Officers of my unit will have maximum time to accomplish their duties; they will not have to accomplish mine. I will earn their respect and confidence as well as that of my soldiers. I will be loyal to those with whom I serve; seniors, peers and subordinates alike. I will exercise initiative by taking appropriate action in the absence of orders. I will not compromise my integrity, nor my moral courage. I will not forget, nor will I allow my comrades to forget that we are professionals, Noncommissioned Officers, leaders!

PIN: 080512-000